Art Treasures of Russia

Art Treasures
of Russia

TEXT BY **M. W. ALPATOV**   *Academy of Fine Arts of the U.S.S.R.*

COMMENTARIES BY **OLGA DACENKO**   *Chief Lecturer, National Museums of France*

HARRY N. ABRAMS, INC. *Publishers* NEW YORK

TRANSLATED BY NORBERT GUTERMAN

Library of Congress Catalog Card Number: 67–12683. All rights reserved. No part of the contents of this book
may be reproduced without the written permission of the publishers HARRY N. ABRAMS, INCORPORATED, NEW YORK

Printed and bound in Japan

This presentation of a panorama

of long-neglected art would have been impossible

without the co-operation of the Soviet Ministry of Culture and

a number of regional authorities in various parts of the Soviet Union.

We are particularly indebted to the technical staffs of the Tretyakov Gallery,

Kremlin Museum, the Russian Museum of Leningrad, and the museums

of Novgorod, Vladimir, Suzdal, Kiev, and Zagorsk. Mr. Halturin

of the Soviet Ministry of Culture provided us with

material that would otherwise have

been unobtainable.

LIST OF PLATES

LIST OF PLATES *continued*

Art Treasures of Russia

ART TREASURES OF RUSSIA

The Italian, Flemish, and Dutch Primitives were discovered and appreciated as early as the first half of the nineteenth century. It took another hundred years for Old Russian art to become known and gain recognition.

In Western Europe, Viollet-le-Duc expressed his admiration for Old Russian churches as early as 1877. Although his hypotheses concerning their Eastern prototypes are scarcely tenable, he was the first to alert France to the existence of this art. In our own day, icon paintings are the most famous treasures of all Russian art. Yet they remained completely unknown for a long time. Not just foreigners but Russians themselves were unable to form any clear idea of Old Russian painting, and without it the general picture of the artistic development of Old Russia remained sketchy.

In Old Russia it was customary to cover icons with an oil that penetrated the pigments and gave them marvelous vigor. As it dried over the centuries, however, this oil turned dark. The icons also picked up dirt and soot, necessitating their being painted over—sometimes several times. Although successive restorations usually preserved the outlines of the original coat of paint, it eventually became impossible to make out the old painting.

1. Cathedral of the Dormition. *1475–79*
Part of the south façade
Kremlin, Moscow

The Cathedral of the Dormition is inside the Kremlin. It was designed by the Bolognese architect Aristotele Fioravanti in accordance with specifications of Ivan the Great, who wanted his capital to have as majestic a church as the five-domed Cathedral of the Dormition in Vladimir.

In 1475, after laying the foundation, Fioravanti went to Vladimir to study the cathedral there. With the help of several Russian architects, he completed the structure in four years.

The Moscow cathedral, with its three naves, five apses (one in the central nave and two in each of the side naves), and five domes, was regarded as the chief cathedral in Russia at that time. It contains the tombs of the metropolitans of Russia.

2. Landscape: *Environs of Novgorod with the Volkhov River*
In the distance, the Church of the Redeemer at Nereditsa. 1198

Early in the twentieth century, such icons began to be restored more scientifically. The topmost layers of darkened oil and inscriptions were now removed with greater care, so that the old paintings were revealed in their original brilliance and beauty. This labor of restoration, and the systematic collecting of Old Russian art, only began to be carried

out on a nationwide scale after the October Revolution. In a decree of 1918, Lenin drew up rules for collecting and preserving the nation's historic monuments. Today such institutions as the Tretyakov Gallery in Moscow and the Russian Museum in Leningrad, as well as a number of provincial museums, contain valuable collections of Old Russian art. The Rublev Museum of Old Russian Art in Moscow was opened on the six-hundredth anniversary of Andrey Rublev, a great artist.

Only when the greatest surviving examples of this art began to be collected and adequately restored did it really begin to be known. Artists were the first to appreciate it, but

art historians were not far behind. Interest in Russian Primitives soon spread beyond the borders of Russia. At present, to quote Roberto Longhi, there is no collector anywhere who does not dream of owning a Rublev icon. However, the present enthusiasm for Russian icon painting does not imply that it is yet widely known or understood. The world of Old Russian icon painting seems fascinating to our contemporaries, but it is far from easily accessible to them.

We run into many obstacles when we attempt to come closer to this art. Many

3. The Archangel Michael. *15th century*
Polychrome wood sculpture, 44½ x 24¼ x 2½"
Museum of Art, Ryazan

Stylistically, this figure is closely related to the icons. Note the slender silhouette, the immense wings that harmonize with the folds of the cloak, and especially the relief treatment. This sculptured icon comes from a church in the village of Putyatino. It is made of prepared lime wood and painted with tempera.

4. *Novgorod workshop:* St. Varlaam of Khutyn
Polychrome wood sculpture. 1560
Novgorod Museum of Art and Architecture

The saint is shown life-size in this painted bas-relief, which was set over a reliquary. His right hand is raised in blessing, and he holds a scroll in his left. The face seems to be a portrait.
   The sculptor was inspired by paintings, but the scale of colors is his own. The vestments were treated with particular care. The prepared wood is painted with tempera.
   The work, which comes from a church in the city of Dmitrov, was made in a Novgorod workshop.

preconceptions prevent us from evaluating it accurately, and the task is the harder the more we confine ourselves to a cursory survey of its treasures.

The first obstacle consists in identifying Old Russian art with Byzantine art, or looking upon it as a mere offshoot of the latter, with local variations. Many art histories treat Old Russian art in the chapter on Byzantium, and sometimes designate it as "Russian Byzantine" or as a "continuation of Byzantine art."

Incontestably, Old Russian art owes a great deal to Byzantium; this is particularly true of its earliest period. Similarly, Italian Renaissance art owes a great deal to ancient Rome, yet no one calls it "Roman." For all its dependence on Byzantine art, Old Russian art differs from it in essential respects. In some instances, it may even be regarded as diametrically opposed. This is best seen when we compare such masters as Theophanes the Greek (plates 32–34, 36) with Rublev (plates 42–47).

Another preconception that gets in the way of understanding is the tendency of Western viewers to look for similarities with late medieval and early Renaissance art. Viewing Old Russian icons, many museum visitors say to themselves: Why, this is quite like Duccio, or Simone Martini, or Sassetta, or Fra Angelico. . . . Such judgments are not entirely unfounded. Martini's charming little *Madonna Annunciata* in the Hermitage does indeed bring to mind the graceful silhouette of the central angel in Rublev's *Trinity* (plate 47). Yet Russian icon painting is fundamentally different. In the case of the Sienese masters, it is obvious that they were all influenced to some extent by the reforms of Giotto; Fra Angelico owes a great deal to Masaccio. The later Sienese artists, for all their poetic charm, are tainted with eclecticism. No such eclecticism appears in Russia until the seventeenth century, under the influence of Western painting. In respect to color, Russian icon painting at its most flourishing period comes closest to the work of Guido da Siena, for he still adhered to Byzantine principles.

Still another way of viewing Old Russian icons is to try to find in them qualities characteristic of the painting of the modern era—motifs derived from real life. It is true that the figures of saints, in certain icons, exhibit features of portraiture; occasionally dukes, warriors, or merchants are shown wearing the dress of their epoch, and their faces express feelings and experiences that the artist could have observed in the faces of contemporaries (military courage, piety, wisdom, etc.). Occasionally also the buildings represented give us some idea of what Old Russian architecture looked like.

On the whole, however, icon painting contains far fewer motifs taken from real life

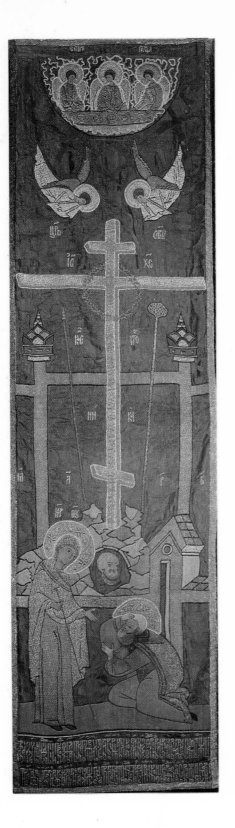

5. *Godunov workshop (attributed):* The Virgin Appearing to St. Sergey
Embroidery. Late 16th century
Trinity-St. Sergey Monastery, Zagorsk

This embroidery, a work of great craftsmanship and exceptional purity of
line, is said to have come from the Godunov workshop. It is made largely of
gold and silver thread, and depicts a large cross with the crown of thorns.
Above the cross is a semicircular glory of the Trinity. At its foot the Virgin
appears to the kneeling St. Sergey. At the bottom is an inscription in very
beautiful Slavonic characters.

than do early Italian or Dutch painting or ancient Greek vase painting. Such motifs appear
in considerable number only when the period of decline sets in. And such late specimens of
Russian icon painting do not give any idea of what it was like in its best period.

One widespread opinion is that Old Russian painting is the ecclesiastical art par

6. The Virgin of Vladimir
Icon. Early 12th century
Egg tempera on wood, 30¾ x 21⅝"
Tretyakov Gallery, Moscow

This work derives from the iconographical type known in Constantinople as the Virgin Eleusa, the Virgin of Mercy and Gentleness. By the middle of the twelfth century, it was known in Russia as *The Virgin of Vladimir*, and was believed to be the protecting spirit of that city.

The icon was brought from Constantinople to Vishgorod, near Kiev, about 1136. In 1155, Prince Andrey Bogolyubsky brought it to Vladimir. In the late fourteenth century, it was taken to the Kremlin in Moscow, but was later brought back to Vladimir. It was installed in the Cathedral of the Dormition in Moscow in 1480. In 1930, it was moved to the Tretyakov Gallery. Early in the fifteenth century, an altar and the instruments of the passion were painted on the back of the panel.

The work has been restored several times. In the fifteenth century the faces were repainted, but the varnish was not removed. This made it possible to restore the original features at a later time.

excellence, and must therefore be evaluated according to corresponding criteria. Now, it is of course undeniable that Old Russian art depended upon and served the Church. But religious subjects alone (study of which is the object of iconography) fail to provide us with the most important elements required for understanding this art. After all, we have an enormous quantity of icons (dating mostly from a later period) that fully come up to ecclesiastical requirements yet have little artistic value. They are a valuable source for our knowledge of iconography but are of no interest to art history. As is well known, the icons of Old Russia were worshiped, were expected to effect cures just like religious relics, were believed to incarnate sacred powers. All this is true, but such forms of worship were only indirectly related to icon painting as an art.

The icons were intended to instruct the faithful, to portray episodes from Holy Scripture, to illustrate the dogmas of the Church. Many icon painters looked upon their work as a sacred duty. But this does not mean that Christian legend and the dogmas of the Church supply the key for understanding the art of the great masters. The artists embodied the people's beliefs—as well as the Church's—in their works, and created legends

The Cathedral of Hagia Sophia is the oldest stone church in Kiev. Its construction was completed in 1037, under Yaroslav the Wise. All that remains of the Church of the Tithe (989–996), built under Prince Vladimir, are the foundations. It was smaller than the cathedral, basilical in form, and had three naves.

Yaroslav the Wise, who greatly enlarged the city of Kiev, had a big cathedral built next to the royal palace. This one originally had five naves and five apses. The cathedral's thirteen domes symbolized Christ and the twelve apostles. The building was pyramidal in form, and a covered gallery ran around three sides.

The cathedral was made of alternating rows of bricks and stone, the latter covered with a pink mortar that, next to the rows of red bricks, produced a polychrome effect. Today the cathedral is white. The shape of the domes was changed in the seventeenth and eighteenth centuries, and the cathedral has undergone other alterations. Only the east façade has been left as it was.

The interior is richly decorated with mosaics and frescoes.

that have no prototype in literary sources. In this they gave free rein to their artistic imagination. They often followed canonic models, the so-called originals. But the most notable fact about masterpieces such as Rublev's *Trinity* (plate 47) is how far they depart from all models. It is in this divergence that the art's creative powers are manifest.

In our own day, Old Russian art, particularly icon painting, evokes still other associations. It is classified as an exotic art, like Negro, pre-Columbian, or Oceanic art. It is also likened to children's art or to that of self-taught painters like Henri Rousseau or Nicco Pirsomanoshvili. It is true that occasional icon paintings strike us as naïve or simple-minded, in expressive power or technique akin to one and another sort of "primitive" art. But taken as a whole this painting marks a maturer stage of artistic development, for it embodies the results of a long historical experience; it is not only youthfully naïve but also expresses centuries-old wisdom.

To our contemporaries, Old Russian art is attractive because it reminds them strangely of modern art—the Fauves, the Cubists, the Surrealists. Henri Matisse spoke

8. Cathedral of Hazia Sophia, Kiev. *1037 Interior (south)*

View through an arch leading from the apse to a side chamber. In the arch the Virgin of the Annunciation is seen, with a series of insets of saints above her.

enthusiastically about Russian icons, saying that those he had seen in Moscow helped him to develop his own artistic idiom. But the harmonious view of the world that lay at the basis of Old Russian art has little in common with the spiritual torments of modern man, and this is why this art is not to be approached in the light of latter-day aesthetic ideas. To approach it this way would merely be to discover points of coincidence in the formal means of expression, and thereby to miss essential differences. Though they help the modern viewer to come closer to the works, judgments of Old Russian art based on first impressions and accidental associations actually divert him from understanding this art in all its uniqueness.

The actual historical background is more important in this connection. Many writers concentrate on certain events of Russian history linked with the creation of this or that work, on the historical figures who commissioned the works or who supported the artists. But far more important than these points of contact between art and history is the fact that

9. Cathedral of Hagia Sophia, Kiev. *1037*
The main apse

In the half dome: the Virgin praying. *Below:* the Communion of the apostles. On each side of the altar stands an angel. Christ is portrayed twice, administering Holy Communion to each group of apostles. *At the level of the windows:* the Fathers of the Church.

On the faces of the arches on either side may be seen the Annunciation—the Archangel Gabriel on the left arch and the Virgin (*see* plate 8) on the right.

Old Russian art as a whole reflects a specific stage in the historical development of the Russian people.

Background to it all was the unification of the eastern Slavs, the founding of the powerful state of Kiev, and the taking of the first steps toward assimilating the ancient culture of the Mediterranean. This was followed by national tragedy, conquest by nomad invaders from the east. Only after long years of Mongol subjection did the principality of Muscovy grow strong enough to secure the freedom and independence of all the eastern Slavs. The fourteenth and fifteenth centuries, when the Russian state was growing by leaps and bounds, marked the culminating point of Old Russian art. It may be said that this art supplied the Russian people with a bright utopian vision with which to light their way through the historical darkness. It was an oath of allegiance to ideals that would live on into the future through many a troubled time.

23

10 and 11. The Fathers of the church. *Mosaic. Cathedral of Hagia Sophia, Kiev. 1037*

This was Russia's springtime, the freshness of which is reflected in the purity and directness of the art it produced. Severe ordeals and the nation's moral strength in meeting them are alike reflected in the art of that time. This was the time when people saw more clearly what ought to be than that which actually was—hence its art contains so many ideal elements. Old traditions served the people as a means of preserving their character, and did not shackle creativity. The people held passionate beliefs, were not afraid to doubt; they sought to know the truth, and many became heretics. Art faithfully mirrored the people's spiritual aspirations. This is why it can still move us today.

Wealth and poverty, happiness and natural disasters, warfare and doctrinal dissension —all these existed at the time but were not reflected in art. The main task of art was to

help man to overcome his spiritual conflicts, to gather his strength, to find his place in the world.

Russian society was feudal. At Novgorod there were struggles among such groups as the boyars, the rich merchants, and the craftsmen. In the monuments of Old Russian art we can observe a difference between the refined art of the upper classes and the poorer, technically inferior, popular or peasant art. At the same time, the art of the feudal elite was not inaccessible to the common people, while peasant art (best known through surviving examples from the northern regions) rested on the same foundations as the art of the upper classes. Apparently the need for unity in face of the common enemy compelled art to aim at universality and general accessibility. The folklore element was very strong—

this is particularly striking in the monuments of Novgorod and Pskov. At the same time, early Russian art does not break down neatly into courtly, chivalric, or burgher categories, as does that of the West in the late Middle Ages.

Like all spiritual culture in the epoch, art was under the sway of the Church. Artists were often members of the clergy, priests or monks. This did not, however, prevent new and fresh elements, created by laymen, from finding their way into art. The shapes of the peasant house (*isba*) influenced the architecture of the churches. The tent-shaped wooden roof was adapted to stone churches, one outstanding example being the famous Church of St. Basil in Moscow (plate 77). In painting, the ideology of the Church, with its monkish renunciation of the world, never wholly dominated: the breath of life found its way into it, giving it warmth and humanity. Only around the middle of the sixteenth century, when the clergy gained strict control, were the links with life broken and the flourishing period of this art brought to an end.

Portrayals of nature, as in landscape, are almost entirely absent from Old Russian painting. But this does not mean that the Russians were indifferent to nature. They expressed the features of their native land, its boundless expanses, which stimulate contemplation and awareness of being part of the world, in the character of their art—above all, in architecture.

Nature in Russia is not striking for its variety or picturesqueness; rather, its charm is like that of the empty Roman Campagna. Even travelers seeing it for the first time cannot be indifferent to it. Russian architecture is above all an architecture of the plain. The Old Russian churches were not erected in crowded towns, like the Gothic cathedrals, nor on steep hillsides, like medieval castles and Georgian churches. Even when situated in towns, they rise against a background of boundless plains and majestically calm rivers.

This mosaic depicting St. Demetrius as a warrior comes from the Cathedral of the Archangel Michael in the monastery of the same name, Kiev, where it occupied the gallery reserved for the reigning prince and his family. The monastery and the church, which was built later, were originally named after St. Demetrius. The founder of the monastery was Prince Izyaslav (son of Yaroslav the Wise, whose daughter, Anna Yaroslavna, married King Henry I of France). His baptismal name was Dmitri, and Demetrius was his patron saint. His son, Prince Svyatopolk II of Kiev, built the first church in 1108–1113.

When Russian architects decorated the exteriors of their churches, they always took into account how the structure would look from afar. The Church of the Intercession (plate 22), on the Nerl River, stands out from a great distance by the whiteness of its harmonious silhouette, but to see its sky-blue stone ornament one must get close to it. The Novgorod churches of the fourteenth and fifteenth centuries rise like friendly lighthouses among the surrounding meadows on the banks of the Volkhov River. The church at Kolomenskoye is inseparable from the hill that rises above the Moskva River where it bends. One can almost believe that it was built on this site so that visitors could admire the beauty of the fields around Moscow from its upper galleries. Birch trees usually stand out harmoniously in a lacy pattern against the white walls of Old Russian monasteries, so that one almost wonders if the architects hadn't built them simply to bring out the beauty of nature.

One of the most attractive features of this architecture is its unpretentiousness. It is as though the builders never strove to surpass the surrounding landscape. On the other hand, they demonstrated their good taste and sense of propriety by making their buildings merge unobtrusively with the surrounding landscape. Unlike Romanesque and Gothic spires, the Russian watchtowers and high bell towers never aim at reaching the sky,

14. Cathedral of Hagia Sophia, Novgorod. *1045–52*

The cathedral was built on the highest elevation of the Kremlin at Novgorod, above the Volkhov River. Originally it had five naves, three apses, and five domes. A sixth dome surmounted the southwest tower, which led to the inner galleries (added in the twelfth century) running around three sides.

The walls were of rather coarse stone, and were covered with pink lime. The arches and vaults were made of brick. The windows were enlarged and redecorated in the seventeenth century. The inside is decorated with frescoes, and there are mosaics in the central apse. On the west façade, above the portal, is a fresco.

never seem to break away from the earth. They remain content to crown the structural mass around them or the adjacent clumps of trees. Universality of form and epic stateliness of idiom define the essential charm of Old Russian architecture. The predilection for fanciful decoration only appears later, when Old Russian art begins to decline.

Just as the churches, thanks to the simplicity of their volumes, are not lost in space, so the Old Russian icon, thanks to its intense coloring and clear forms, is not lost within the interior dimness of the church. When a candle is lighted in front of it, its brilliant colors seem to conquer the surrounding darkness. Therein is implied the characteristic philosophy of this art, which modern man finds so hard to grasp. Many believe that it is always turning away from reality, some criticizing this as a shortcoming, others praising it and calling it "transcendence." The fact is that Old Russian art was always turned toward humanity, life, reality. The Old Russian icon is not so much a representation, a duplication of the already existing, as a creation shaped by the artist according to the laws of beauty, a creation from which light and joy emanate. The artist brought it into the human world to give mankind joy and to slake its thirst for the beautiful.

Russian architecture of the eighteenth and early nineteenth centuries is very similar to the architecture of other European countries in the same period. A painting by a modern Russian artist can most often be distinguished from a painting of the French or German school only with reference to extraneous features, the details of the human figures

or of the scenery. With the exception of the very oldest works influenced by Byzantium,
a Russian icon is far more readily distinguishable from other pictures on religious subjects.
A Russian church, for all its general canonic type, will never be confused with a Byzantine,
Serbian, or Georgian church. It is impossible to define the hallmarks of the Russian style in a
few words, but the eye detects them easily.

The Church of the Intercession on the Nerl (plate 22), or the Novgorod icon *St. George
and the Dragon* (plate 54), could have been created only in Russia. They provide an
occasion for pondering what the *genius loci* means in art, what part is played in art by the
national character.

Many different schools of art, many different artistic tendencies existed in Old Russia.
But there was also always something they had in common, no matter where produced
over the vast stretches of that boundless land. It is easy to distinguish a Russian icon from
the icons of other eastern European countries, whether Byzantine, Serbian, or Ukrainian.
Each bears the imprint of the Russian style of icon painting, and this is true even of
the most unassuming works.

Old Russian art is a deeply humane art. It has something of the warmth characteristic
of Russian folk poetry. The spiritual tenor of Old Russian art is usually calm and cheerful.
We find in it no states of elation to the point of ecstasy, no gloomy despair, no

St. Nicholas, the most venerated of the Russian saints, is the protector of the outcast. He is also called the Miracle Worker. The saint holds the Gospel in his left hand, which is covered with one edge of his priestly vestment, a sign of veneration. The figure has a monumental quality that is both expressive and subtle.

In the thirteenth century, the figures of ten other saints, among them two other miracle workers, SS. Cosmas and Damian, were added on the white edges that originally served as a frame around the central figure.

According to a tradition of the Novodevichi Monastery in Moscow, the icon was brought from Novgorod in 1564 by Ivan the Terrible, who gave it to the monastery along with the icon *The Panagia Virgin*.

expressions of sinfulness and hopelessness. This is reflected not only in the facial expressions (which as a rule are what we notice first) but in the art itself. True, Old Russian paintings often express sorrow and suffering, but even then the spiritual poise is not shattered. In their icons of the Mother of God fondling the Child, the Old Russian masters succeeded particularly well in touching the viewer's heart. These works were collectively referred to as *umilenye* ("compassionate," "tender"), for this was the feeling they communicated. But Old Russian painting is never sentimental; its austerity did not relax to the point of indulging human weakness.

Joyousness always pervades these works, puts a special stamp on them. The modern viewer may find this strange: after all, these works were created in times of extreme hardship; the chronicles of the period speak of little but calamity and misfortune. Art simply passed everyday experience by, as though not noticing it. Its task was to meet man's need for something elevated, luminous, good, to uplift him and awaken nobler feelings in him. These feelings are expressed particularly clearly in icons on the theme of the ancient hymn to the Virgin, "All Living Things Rejoice in Thee," which was much favored by the Old Russian masters.

Joyousness filled these works, first, because at that time man did not feel alone in the

17. Christ Emmanuel between the Archangels Michael and Gabriel
Icon-deësis. Mid-12th century
Egg tempera, 28⅜ x 50¾″
Tretyakov Gallery, Moscow

In its iconography, this work recalls the seventh and eighth centuries, at which time the three figures were sometimes replaced by their initials. Closest to the old style is the figure of Christ Emmanuel.

The Greek word *deësis* stands for prayer, supplication. There are several kinds of deëses. Christ is always in the middle. Turned toward Him on either side in supplication are the Virgin and St. John the Baptist; the latter are often replaced by the archangels Michael and Gabriel, or by SS. Peter and Paul; other saints are sometimes added.

Deësis figures may be full length or may be represented by the bust or head alone.

From the twelfth to the fourteenth centuries, the deësis was placed above the tsar's door, above the west portal of religious buildings, and above the entrance door of secular buildings. The deësis was also used in the composition of icons on a complex subject, for example the Last Judgment.

The present icon is in rather poor condition. The layers of paint have undergone many changes. The halos, originally pink, are hardly visible, and the gilded background has almost completely disappeared. The archangels are wearing diadems adorned with red stones set in gold. According to Old Russian texts, these *toroki* indicate the dwelling place of the Holy Ghost.

world (modern man suffers from this feeling). He always felt himself to be the member of a community, a particle in the larger life of mankind. Nor did he know many of the contradictions familiar to modern Western man. The view that suffering is divine only came in with the Reformation and the Counter Reformation, as many works of the period illustrate. In Russian painting, it is joy that is divine; the attitude is closer to that of the ancient Greeks, who worshiped the gods of Olympus.

To the extent that Russian icon painting sought to portray man as participating in a universal harmony, it passed over in silence the contradictions that had not yet been resolved. Harmony, the sense of measure, of balance—these are clearly reflected in icon composition. In no other art of medieval Europe are the principles of Greek eurythmy asserted as clearly as in Old Russian icon painting; on this score the Russian masters are rivaled only by those of the Italian Renaissance. Everything shown in these icons is clearly outlined,

easily taken in by the eye. The surface of the wooden panel is usually articulated
according to simple arithmetic ratios. The icon painter subordinates the parts to the whole,
never lets them get out of hand.

Rhythm plays a particularly important part in this art, and all the masters disclose
great sensitivity on this score. Rhythms are stressed by repetitions of the same motif
or by its regular alternation with other recurrent motifs. The Novgorod school stresses the
architectural principle of composition; the Moscow school, particularly in the works
of Rublev and his followers, emphasizes the musical principle. In the Novgorod icon
St. George and the Dragon (plate 54), the round contours of the warrior, the horse's head, and
the shield are repeated three times, and they are arranged one above the other like the arches
of a building. In Rublev's *Trinity* (plate 47), too, the rounded contours are repeated,
but here they are more flexible, more flowing and melodious.

18. *School of Novgorod (attributed)*: The Holy Face
Icon. *12th century. Egg tempera on wood, 30¼ x 28"*
Tretyakov Gallery, Moscow

The style of this work is monumental. The painter used a Byzantine or Kievan model. The treatment is spare, the Veronica's Veil motif reduced to an abstract schema. The face of Christ appears in a circular inset with a cross. The expression of the eyes is deeply human, a characteristic of Russian art.

At the bottom left is a wax seal with the arms of the Cathedral of the Dormition in the Moscow Kremlin, where the icon was originally kept.

The back of the panel shows an adoration of the Cross by the archangels Michael and Gabriel.

One characteristic of Russian icon painting is the correlation between organic and abstract geometric forms. The adherence to abstract geometric forms may be a survival of the ancient Slavic art of signs. But in icon painting the abstract forms are not in contradiction with the organic structure of the human body. The artists aim at reconciling the two principles. As a result, they favor those organic forms that can be expressed with the help of regular geometric forms. Rublev's *Trinity*, for example, can be inscribed in a circle, and the same is true of the heads of the angel and of St. Paul in Zvenigorod. Motifs of this kind are found both in portrayals of individual figures and in scenes with many figures. This peculiarity of the Old Russian painterly way of seeing may be defined as a striving to reconcile the real and the ideal, existence and aspiration. The Old Russian masters sought to transpose reality to a domain governed by higher laws.

In painting, the outlines indicate not only the boundaries of objects but also the direction of their movement, the forces they express. The impetuous movement of St. George's horse is rendered by the powerful curve of its neck. To express man's spiritual qualities, the masters shortened his extremities—the arms and legs, the head. The bodies are less elongated than in Gothic art, and for this reason they retain their corporeal quality. But the inner force emanating from them breaks through the boundaries of the contours. Dionysius' warrior figures (plates 62, 63) have narrow, thin bodies; their physical strength

19. Cathedral of St. George. *1119–30*
Vicinity of Novgorod

In its austerity and lovely proportions, the Cathedral of St. George, in the Yuriev (George) Monastery, is one of the finest surviving Old Russian structures. Situated on the left bank of the Volkhov River, it dominates the landscape around it. Designed with great simplicity by the architect Pyotr, it has three naves, three apses, and three domes. One of the domes rises above a square tower with a stairway from the inner galleries. The inner walls, like those of the tower, were once decorated with frescoes.

is invisible, so to speak, but we sense their spiritual power. A similar pictorial treatment marks the rendering of inanimate objects, motifs from buildings, and landscapes.

We cannot agree with the widespread opinion that the treatment of space in Old Russian painting is accounted for by the Russian masters' ignorance of Brunelleschi's discoveries. These masters, it is true, were unacquainted with scientific perspective, but, unlike the Italian masters of the *trecento*, they were not in search of it. To call their perspective "inverted" does not cast any light on it. The space that figures in Old Russian painting is of a special kind, but it never so much as hints at some single point of convergence. Modern viewers familiar with the Cubist experiments will find their way to an understanding of this pictorial space more readily than viewers of earlier periods. Houses, objects, or rocky mountains in Old Russian painting always have a certain spatial quality, but they never recede into depth; instead, they come forward from the picture plane to form a separate zone. In the icon *The Entombment* (plate 55), the sarcophagus containing the body of Christ in its winding sheet comes forward a little. In the icons and murals of Dionysius there is more depth, but it is not distinctly defined—Giotto's "boxlike" space was unknown to him. The Old Russian masters were very sensitive to the role of space between bodies. It plays no less a part in the composition of icons than the bodies themselves, and this is why everything represented is kept within the pictorial plane.

It is impossible to speak of this art without touching on its brilliant colors. The coloring

Iconographically this work goes back to an ancient Eastern model. The Christ Child is against the Virgin's bosom. In Old Russian texts the Virgin is called "The Virgin of the Incarnation." The angel originally may not have had wings, in keeping with an old iconographic tradition. The present wings were added when the painting was restored in the sixteenth century.

The icon comes from the Cathedral of the Dormition in the Moscow Kremlin. In 1561, according to the *Chronicles of Novgorod,* Ivan the Terrible had the "Annunciation of the Yuriev Monastery" brought to Moscow from the Cathedral of Hagia Sophia in Novgorod.

The icon may have been painted when the Cathedral of St. George in the Yuriev Monastery was founded, in the first half of the twelfth century, during the reign of Prince Vsevolod Gabriel Mstislavovich. The archangel Gabriel was the prince's patron saint.

The name Ustyug has been attached to the work, probably because of a legend that the icon was brought to Moscow from the city of that name in the middle of the sixteenth century. However, the legend is not supported by any reliable document.

of the icons has a unique fascination, which captivates even viewers to whom the spiritual world of icon painting is alien and incomprehensible. With respect to composition of the individual scenes, the masters were confined by tradition to a certain number of types or models that had been passed on from generation to generation. They had greater opportunity to express their originality in the coloring, and they managed to say in colors far more than can be said in words. Their colors are now vigorous, now tender; now we enjoy their beauty, now we are stirred by their passionate intensity; they express both joy of life and profound feeling. Often the coloring enables us to ascribe an icon to a school or century. The Old Russian icons differ from the nobly restrained but somewhat more gloomily colored Byzantine icons by their bright, clear, pure colors. But the pigment itself is never stressed; it is subordinated to the spiritual impression of the whole. Not a single spot of color ever conflicts with the overall scale of color. The interplay of colors animates and spiritualizes the icons.

21. Cuff of a vestment
Embroidery. 12th century
Novgorod Museum of Art and Architecture

Under semicircular arches between two strips with floral ornamentation are the three figures of the deësis. Christ is in the middle, the Virgin on the left, and St. John the Baptist on the right.

Like their Western contemporaries, the Old Russian masters aimed at color harmony. But in the fifteenth century the requirement of rendering local colors came to the fore, and as a result it was difficult to achieve that "friendship of colors" advocated by L. B. Alberti. The Old Russian masters were not restricted in their treatment of color: they were free to paint any object in whatever color they chose. We find blue horses, red mountains, multicolored buildings and costumes such as never existed, and grounds either golden or bright red. With such freedom, color harmony could always be achieved. In Russian icons the colors rarely have a conventional allegorical meaning—their meaning is defined by the overall impression, the coloring of the whole.

Color in icons is always the vehicle of a specific expressivity—this reflects its human significance. That is not to say, however, that it expresses the artist's personal mood. The dominant concern in icon painting is to make coloring accord with the generally accepted and generally understood. Rublev's *Trinity* is remarkable for its beautiful, clear colors, and we can infer its creator's taste from it; yet when this work formed part of the iconostasis in the Trinity-St. Sergey Monastery (Troitse-Sergeyeva Lavra), it fitted into the color harmony of the whole and formed an inseparable part of it. The border scenes in the icon of the *Metropolitan Alexey* by Dionysius (plate 59) can be viewed individually, but when we view the icon as a whole they blend together to make a beautiful ornamental design, a sort of wreath of flowers around the standing saint.

Although the Russian master painters made the most of the properties of color, the pigment never takes on the importance it has in modern impasto painting. The colors of icons

According to tradition, the site of the church was chosen by Prince Andrey Bogolyubsky in memory of his son Izyaslav, who died fighting the Bulgarians. During the same period, a new feast of the Virgin, the Intercession, was established by the clergy of Vladimir. Everything about this church, which was dedicated to the Virgin and built in memory of a young prince, gives an impression of purity and perfection. One is surprised, at first, by the choice of site. Even today the mound raised to protect the church is flooded in spring.

Several reconstructions have been offered by archaeologists. The mound originally had a stone facing, and monumental steps led to the entrance of the church. A magnificent gallery used to run around three sides of the church. In the time of Bogolyubsky, the Nerl, a tributary of the Klyazma, which with the Oka and the Volga formed a major river system, was the route leading to Suzdal. Boats from Suzdal and Rostov, carrying ambassadors and visitors from the East, sailed past the church.

In keeping with an old Vladimir-Suzdal architectural tradition, the church has only one dome. It has three apses. The restrained decoration of the façades, with small, slender inset columns that accentuate the church's elegant outline, is characteristic of the region.

The roof and the dome have been altered.

affect us powerfully. When we look at them, it is as though we are seeing color for the first time; we feel joy in life, a higher world becomes accessible to us. This is why the discovery of icon painting early in this century produced such a strong impression. Modern man was confronted with an art in which color, freed from external conditions, achieves the fullest possible expression.

In Old Russian painting, color is always associated with light. In the icons, light never falls on the colored surface of the object as it does in fourteenth-century Byzantine icons; rather, the light penetrates the colors, as it does to some extent in Gothic stained-glass windows. It is possible to speak here of "light-color," for here the two elements are inseparable. In the Novgorod icons the ground and the objects are often rendered in the same color. But, depending on the context, it produces a different impression. In disposing the spots of color, the masters followed the same laws that governed their disposition of objects: they aimed at wholeness, balance, rhythm, two-dimensionality, harmony.

This orant is known in Russia as "The Great Panagia." (The term orant refers to the attitude of the figure, with arms outstretched as in prayer.) The Virgin is shown with an inset of the Christ Child on her bosom. The icon, which recalls the famous picture of the Virgin in the Church of the Blachernai in Constantinople, has also been called "The Virgin of the Annunciation."

Kept in Yaroslavl since the eighteenth century, this work was attributed to the school of that city. However, the monumental style, the gilded mosaiclike decoration, and the Hellenistic quality of the two angels were also characteristic of masterpieces of the school of Kiev.

The *Chronicles of the Lavra (Monastery) of Kiev* ascribe a "large icon of the Virgin" to the painter Alimpi Pechersky, a monk who died in 1114. This icon has sometimes been identified with *The Panagia Virgin.* Perhaps it was sent to Rostov the Great in the twelfth century, during the reign of Prince Vladimir Monomakh of Kiev. When the archbishopric was transferred to Yaroslavl in 1788, the icon was taken to the new residence in the Monastery of the Transfiguration, where it was discovered in 1919.

No matter what subject the icons represent, their open, bright, radiant tones endow them with joyful, festive color, a glow of pure beauty. The icons of the best period give the human eye the joy that, according to Delacroix, is an attribute of genuine painting. The Old Russian masters came close to the ideal of pure painting that modern artists pursue in the so-called art of collage. The icons have a quality that can be expressed only in color, something that cannot be found anywhere else.

Many collectors of icons, and authors of scholarly works on them as well, value them primarily for their technical qualities. These essentially superficial qualities hold their attention to such a point that they forget the main thing, that the finest icons are genuine works of art. To be sure, the icons can be used as a source for the study of Russian history, the character of the Russian people, their religious ideas, etc. But these works are so valuable primarily because they are true works of art; it is primarily in this capacity that they are accessible and comprehensible to us, that they can be a source of pure and noble

24. St. Demetrius of Salonika *(detail)*
Icon. 12th century, second half
Egg tempera on wood
Tretyakov Gallery, Moscow

The saint has the bearing of a warrior prince. He is sitting on a sumptuous throne, and his sword, symbol of his power, is half-drawn from its scabbard.

An oral tradition of the city of Dmitrov (in the Moscow area), where the icon was discovered in 1919, links the work with Grand Duke Vsevolod Dmitri of the Big Brood (so called because he had a large number of children). Dmitrov was a fortified town founded in 1154 by Prince Yuri Dolgoruky in celebration of the birth of his son Vsevolod Dmitri.

Prince Yuri Ivanovich (1504–1533) rebuilt the old twelfth-century cathedral and dedicated to St. George, his patron saint, the church that formerly had borne the name of St. Demetrius of Salonika. The icon comes from this twelfth-century church.

enjoyment for modern man. However literally the icons were worshiped by contemporaries of the artists who created them, people who ascribed a mysterious healing power to them, to us they are art above all else.

We know virtually nothing about how these masterpieces were appreciated by their first viewers. The statements on art to be found in Old Russian sources are very brief. But judging by the masters they most valued, by the particular icons recognized as especially sacred, we may infer that their first viewers keenly appreciated the icon painters' artistry.

Old Russian painting is always a representational art. It does not depict everyday objects, however, but objects that, according to the ideas of the epoch, hold in themselves the essence of the world. We must suppose that these masters were able to discover this essence through their art, and then we will not be surprised that although we recognize real objects in the icons, they have been transfigured.

The world of Old Russian icon painting fascinates us by its intrinsic harmony, to the point where we may recognize that it was a better world than the one we live in. The modern viewer who looks upon this world from outside, perhaps with a feeling of superiority, might suppose

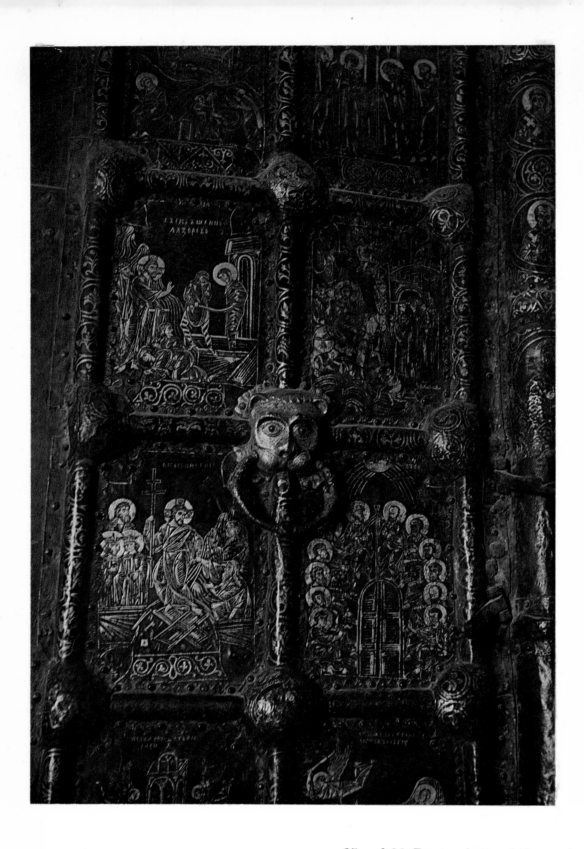

25 and 26. Bronze doors of the west portal. *1230–33*
Cathedral of the Nativity of the Virgin, Suzdal. 1222–25

The west portal of the Cathedral of the Nativity of the Virgin was made by goldsmiths from Vladimir and Suzdal. This part of the church was directly opposite the prince's residence. The portal, which is known as the Golden Door, contains twenty-eight scenes arranged in two vertical columns on the two doors. Each door, of gold applied on a dull bronze surface, has floral ornamentation and a magnificent lion's head with a ring.

The work is technically perfect. Together, the doors form one immense icon surmounted with a semicircular spandrel and decorated with insets painted in fresco showing the deësis. The scene of the Intercession of the Virgin is thought to be the oldest depiction of the theme in Russian art.

The details reproduced here include seven of the scenes: from left to

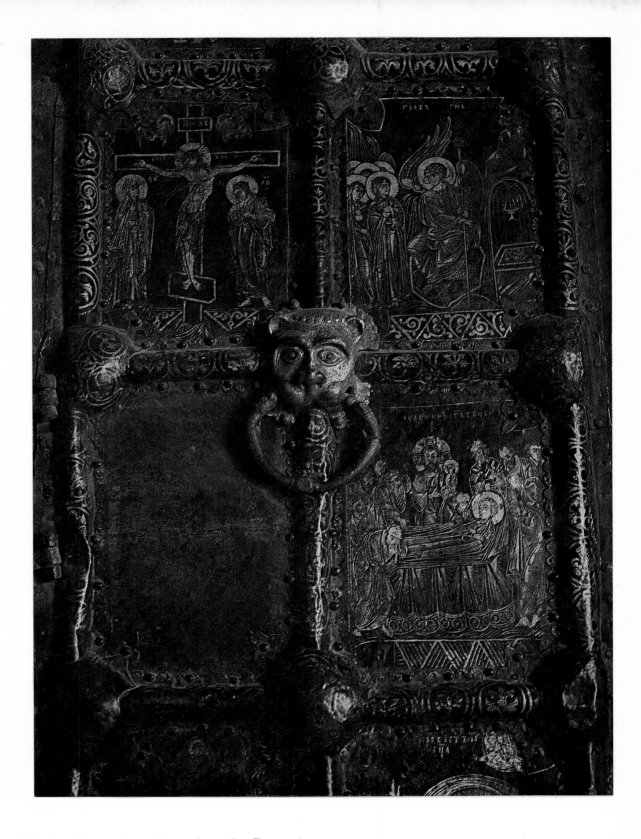

right, the Raising of Lazarus, Christ's Entry into Jerusalem, the Descent into Limbo, the Descent of the Holy Ghost, the Crucifixion, the Women at the Tomb, and the Dormition of the Virgin. On all these scenes are inscriptions in Slavonic that make this work an important source for the study of paleography.

This portal was commissioned by Bishop Mitrofan (1227–1238) and includes a depiction of his patron saint. The bishop died hideously when the Tatars burned the Cathedral of the Dormition in Vladimir.

The south portal, consecrated to the archangel Michael, protector of the princes of Russia, was commissioned by Prince Yuri Vasilievich and executed in the same period.

An inventory of 1609 mentions a bishop's pulpit (since vanished) also executed in gilded bronze, a large collection of liturgical objects, and Limoges enamels that were brought from France by Russian travelers.

that the icon masters looked upon their creations merely as "offspring of their pious imaginations." In actual fact, their attitude was very different. They wholeheartedly believed in the real existence of their world, and it is precisely that unshakable faith that accounts for the icons' powerful appeal. Modern man, who has learned to doubt everything, and who thinks everything is relative, finds special gratification at being presented here with something as incontrovertible as an axiom.

The Old Russian masters were as trusting and sincere as children. At the same time, icon painting reflects the accumulated experience of many centuries, going back to ancient Byzantium. Unlike Byzantine art, however, which never reflects any life outside the walls of church and monastery, Russian painting gives expression to the moral questions that were preoccupying all men in that period. Russian painting is less sensuous than many works of the Constantinople school, but it also lacks the severe asceticism characteristic of the art of Sinai and Athos. The Russian icons contain reflections of a purely human and secular beauty, and in this respect the fifteenth-century icons bring to mind altarpieces of the early Italian Renaissance, which similarly introduced into the half-light of church interiors a glimmer of the light that was then filling the whole world.

In one essential respect, however, Russian icon painting differs from the late medieval and Renaissance art of the West. There, art enjoyed the quickening influence of a developing secular philosophy and mathematical science. Old Russian icon painting did not benefit from or compete with science, nor was it influenced by rationalism. In it, art alone holds sway,

Many icon painters were inspired by two texts from the first Book of Kings, particularly the following: ". . . he went and dwelt by the brook Cherith, that is before Jordan. And the ravens brought him bread . . ."

The present work, however, illustrates the second of these texts: "Go forth, and stand upon the mount before the Lord. And, behold, the Lord passed by, and a great and strong wind rent the mountains, and brake in pieces the rocks before the Lord; but the Lord was not in the wind . . . a still small voice. And it was so, when Elijah heard it, that he wrapped his face in his mantle, and went out, and stood in the entering in of the cave. And, behold, there came a voice unto him, and said, What doest thou here, Elijah?" The icon shows Elijah listening to the "still small voice."

The delicate coloring heightens the old man's attentive look as he cups his ear. Around the border are scenes from the prophet's life. At the top we have an especially full deësis: Christ, in the middle, is flanked by the Virgin, John the Baptist, St. Peter, and St. Paul.

The icon comes from the Church of the Prophet Elijah in the village of Vybuty, near Pskov. According to a local tradition, the village was the birthplace of Princess Olga (reigned 945–955), the only female ruler of Russia before the eighteenth century.

everything is achieved by a poetic apprehension of the world, through intuition, the basis of faith in human feeling and imagination. This is not to say that Russian icon painting contains no wisdom of its own. It has considerable depth, and modern man often must call upon all his intellectual resources to gain insight into it.

Old Russia inherited from Byzantium the ancient conception of the symbol as the foundation of artistic imagery. In addition to its obvious meaning, every figure in the icon has its special connotations. This doctrine was also known in the West. But Gothic art was dominated by a strictly rationalistic allegorizing—every object designated some specifically defined other object. In Russian icon painting the second meaning is merely implied: we merely sense its presence behind the visible forms. Every image includes a whole range of meanings, not fully conscious but intuitively divined.

This conception of the symbol brought about an enlarging of the narrow schemata of

This icon was found in the monastery church of Tolgsk, near Yaroslavl. There are various hypotheses concerning its origin. An old chronicle mentions an icon of the Virgin that was brought in 1278 from Georgia by Prince Fyodor Rostislavovich the Black, who had fought there. It may have been the work that is reproduced here. If so, it was painted before 1278. Certainly the fact that *The Tolgsk Virgin* is painted on cypress wood tends to prove that the icon was not made in Russia. This is a further argument for its Georgian origin.

Pictures of the Virgin Hodegetria ("She who leads") were widespread in Georgia. The theme of the Virgin Eleusa (the Virgin of Gentleness) with the Child, the subject of the present work, was a variant. In the fourteenth century, the school of Yaroslavl produced other variants of this Georgian icon.

ecclesiastical iconography. The Russian masters obediently reproduced traditional iconographic motifs, portraying the saints and the principal events in the Christian calendar. But through this outer crust there invariably transpires a new conception of the fundamental problems involved in the relations between heaven and earth, man's place in such a world, and the fate he may expect—problems that were much stirring mankind at the time.

Rublev's *Trinity* shows only three figures, but it reflects a profound conception of the structure and principle of the universe. In portraying feasts of the Church and scenes from the lives of the saints, the Old Russian masters followed Holy Writ but did not limit themselves to illustrating it. They created visual symbols almost untranslatable into the language of words and abstract notions, yet which convey profound meanings. The icon painters were genuine creative artists. By no means all modern artists are capable of as great a depth of vision.

The creative torments that are the lot of many talented artists in our day were unknown to the icon painters. They believed firmly that they could express in their art everything they felt. But we must not suppose that they were unaware of the possibility of failure, that they never experimented. Although these artists followed their traditional "originals," they

30. *School of Moscow:* SS. Boris and Gleb on Horseback
Icon. c.1340. Egg tempera on wood
Tretyakov Gallery, Moscow

The princes Boris and Gleb, sons of Vladimir I, the canonized Prince of
Kiev (980–1015), are shown on horseback. Their martyrdom (violent
death in a fratricidal struggle with Svyatopolk) is symbolized by the halos
around their heads and by the presence of Christ, who is blessing them, at
the upper right.

The icon comes from the Chapel of SS. Peter and Paul in the Cathedral
of the Dormition in the Moscow Kremlin.

The cult of SS. Boris and Gleb was established in the middle of the
eleventh century by Yaroslav the Wise, their elder brother, who had become Prince of Kiev. A life of the saints was written in the same period.
In the middle of the twelfth century, Prince Andrey Bogolyubsky built the
Church of SS. Boris and Gleb at Kideksha, near Suzdal. In 1948, frescoes
representing the two saints on horseback were discovered on the inner
walls of the church. These frescoes are thought to date from the time the
church was built.

continually departed from their models, and success depended on their inspiration. This
becomes clear when we study different icons treating the same subject. For instance,
comparison between Rublev's *Trinity* and one by an anonymous contemporary of his (plate
49) suffices to show the difference between a work of genius and a work by an average master.
Rublev solved a problem with which his predecessors had long struggled in vain. Ordinary
painters adhered closely to tradition, venturing to depart from it only in matters of detail.

We know very little about the founders of Old Russian art—even less than about the
builders of the Gothic cathedrals. Judging by the surviving works, they included skilled
artisans, expert masters, and finally geniuses such as Rublev, Dionysius, and the
Master of the Kremlin.

Only a fraction of Old Russian art has come down to us, and this book contains
reproductions of but a small part of the works now in the museums of the Soviet Union. These
examples should, however, convey some idea of what this art was like as a whole. A brief survey
of its development will contribute to our understanding of it.

St. Basil's Church, which has only one dome, is harmoniously proportioned. One of the characteristics of Pskov architecture is the use of stone for geometrical decoration. The roughness of the stone gives the whitewashed outer walls of this and other small churches an irregularity of surface that has great charm. The roof and windows were altered in the seventeenth and eighteenth centuries.

The earliest period extends over the eleventh and twelfth centuries. This was the period of the powerful state of Kiev, of rulers such as Vladimir Monomakh and Yaroslav the Wise, a period during which Byzantine culture began to spread into Russia. In the twelfth century, this state broke up into small principalities, and new cultural centers sprang up, particularly in the northeast. Cut off from commercial contacts with the rest of the world as a result of the Crusades, Russia became a wholly agricultural country. Internecine wars between the dukes ravaged the land. The epic *Tale of Prince Igor* celebrates the valor of the duke and his warriors, and the beauty of their native land. Many persons at this time took refuge in monasteries.

The dukes of Kiev, and later the dukes of Vladimir and the boyars of Novgorod, imported Byzantine works of art and extended invitations to Greek artists to come to Russia. Chroniclers of the eleventh century refer to a Russian artist, Alimpi Pechersky.

The oldest monument of Russian architecture is the Cathedral of Hagia Sophia in Kiev (plates 7–12), which has impressive mosaics and frescoes. A cruciform church in the Byzantine manner, it was designed by Byzantine architects and decorated with mosaics by Byzantine artists. But it has thirteen domes—churches with so many domes are almost never encountered in former Byzantine territories. The use of many domes, a frequently remarked characteristic of later Russian churches, may reflect the influence of native Russian wooden buildings. The conception of the church as unifying point of the city and of the land as a whole is expressed in the pyramidal silhouette of the Kiev cathedral (plate 7), and is partly

32. *Theophanes the Greek*
" Old Testament Trinity" (Abraham and Sarah Entertaining the Angels)
Fresco. 1378
Cathedral of the Transfiguration of the Redeemer, Novgorod

The frescoes were commissioned by Prince Vasily Danilovich and the residents of St. Elijah Street, where the church (completed in 1374) was located. *The Chronicles of Novgorod*, which mention the name of the painter, say that the frescoes were done in the summer of 1378.

We know that Theophanes came to Novgorod when he was about forty. He left Constantinople in 1370 after a stay in Caffa, which was then a Genoese colony in the Crimea. Theophanes, who was brought up in the neo-Hellenistic aesthetic tradition of the Paleologues, was not only a very original and gifted painter but also a philosopher. He may have been familiar with the doctrine of the Hesychasts. His paintings reflect their teachings concerning the light of the transfigured Christ on Mount Tabor, the spiritual power of that divine light, and how it was transmitted to mankind. The writer Epiphanius, his contemporary, called him "a wise man and a profound thinker."

The cathedral is in the form of a cross and has only one dome. The frescoes, which are quite extensive, were later covered with whitewash. They were not rediscovered until 1910, and restoring them went on until 1944 and beyond. The parts now visible are in the drum of the dome, the most beautiful and best preserved in the diaconicon in the upper part of the church. On one of the walls of the diaconicon is the *Trinity;* on the other (in inset) are frescoes of St. Acacius, St. Macarius, and the pillar saints.

Theophanes gives a traditional interpretation of the Trinity (Genesis 18:1–10). Around the altar are the three angels. In the right foreground is Sarah. The figure of Abraham, who was at the left, has disappeared. The originality of the scene lies in the painter's personal style. The wings of the middle angel are spread across the entire scene.

The dominant color of these frescoes is red ocher. Theophanes also used streaks of brilliant white, the purpose of which was not to achieve chiaroscuro effects but rather a certain expressionism peculiar to his style. The range is completed by muted tones of blue, green, pink, and yellow, which produce a delicate harmony.

preserved in the Novgorod Cathedral of Hagia Sophia (plate 14), which dates from the eleventh and twelfth centuries, with its massive walls and six mighty, closely crowded domes.

The interior of Kiev's Hagia Sophia was covered from floor to ceiling with mosaics and wall paintings. From the skylighted dome the Pantocrator looks sternly down, holding the Book of the Law. He is surrounded by winged youths, the heavenly host, and the archangels. Below them, on the piers between twelve windows, rise the apostles, and below

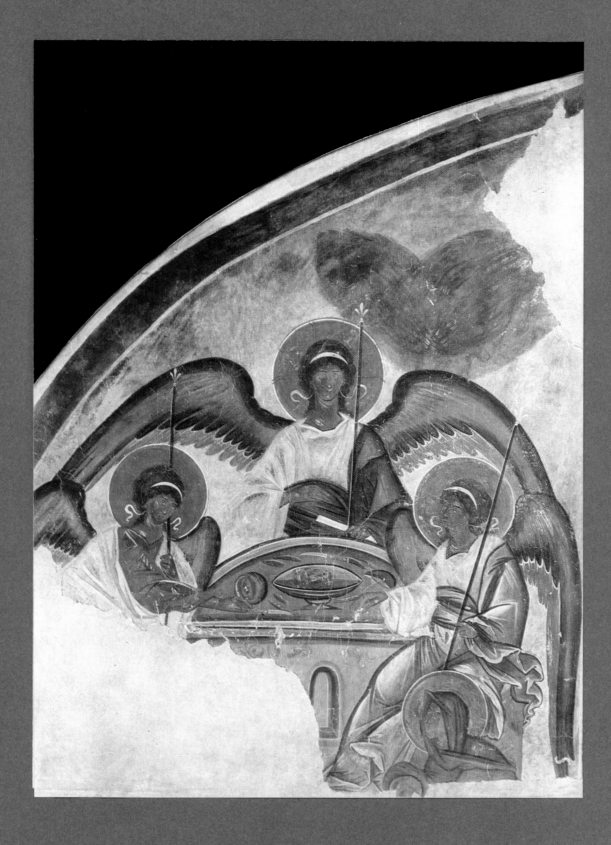

these the four Evangelists. Above the altar is the immense figure of the Virgin with raised arms, begging the Pantocrator to be merciful to mankind. This Madonna of Kiev was known as *The Indestructible Wall*. On the altar is a representation of Christ giving the sacrament to His disciples, and under it a solemn row of Fathers of the Church.

With figures of saints and martyrs all around them, the Russians of the period familiarized themselves with the heavenly hierarchy, which was intended to strengthen the authority of the feudal hierarchy here on earth. Not for nothing were the figures of the duke and his family included among the decorations. All these stately figures seem to surround the viewer from all sides, making him feel that he is present among them. Here is embodied the idea of communal action that we find expressed in later Russian icons, particularly those on the subject of divine intercession.

The mosaic *St. Demetrius* from the Mikhailov Monastery at Kiev (plate 13) is a vivid, profoundly human portrait of a warrior and at the same time a specimen of the subtlest color treatment. Warm tones, such as pink and gold, are harmonized with cold blue, green, and neutral grays. The armor is gold, like the ground, but stands out from it, thanks to the dark blue contours. The white band on the chest, with its blue shadows, has the same luminosity to be found in Impressionist paintings.

The oldest Byzantine painting in Russia is *The Virgin of Vladimir* (plate 6), which went from Constantinople to Kiev and to Vladimir, where it became a local shrine. The restorers

had to remove seven layers of paint before the faces of the Virgin and Child were revealed to us in all their original beauty. Among the finest monuments of Byzantine painting, the beauty of this icon is unrivaled. It is one of the noblest images of motherhood in world art. It served as a starting point for the development of the Russian school—the subject of motherly tenderness was a favorite with the Old Russian masters. The Vladimir Madonna shows many purely Byzantine features. Her enormous eyes express sorrow at the future sufferings of her Son and address a silent reproach to the world. Executed in the subtlest light and shadow in complementary tones, this icon is striking in its vivid corporeality like nearly all works of late

34. *Theophanes the Greek*
St. Macarius
Fresco. 1378
Cathedral of the Transfiguration of the Redeemer, Novgorod

St. Macarius the Egyptian, an anchorite who preached the discipline of silence, was particularly venerated by the Hesychasts. He is shown in an attitude of prayer, and seems to be entirely clothed in his long white hair.

classical painting, yet the spiritual element is victorious over the material: it is no accident that the almond-shaped eyes are larger than the thin mouth.

In the twelfth century, Russian icon masters were strongly influenced by mural painting. Icons were executed on large wooden panels, the figures often more than life-size. Icons that big are almost never found in Byzantium. In Russia they were intended to serve in the stead of mosaics and frescoes. At this time most of the icons represented standing figures turned toward the viewer, their facial expressions severe and tense. The colors were saturated, dark, with gold grounds, and often the figures were outlined in gold as well—this minimized the differences between icons and mosaics.

Local schools had not yet grown up. It is conjectured that some icons executed in Kiev turned up later in northern Russia. It is harder to distinguish a Novgorod icon from one found in Vladimir-Suzdal than a Novgorod church from a Vladimir-Suzdal church.

In the deësis from the Cathedral of the Dormition in Moscow (plate 17), where it was placed near *The Virgin of Vladimir*, the facial expressions of all three figures are stern and tense. The child bears himself like an adult, and the scrawny angels stare at him. The prayerful unity that was later to become the characteristic feature of Russian deësis icons is missing here. The coloring is gloomy, the faces muddy, and only the delicate pink clothing and the bright red jewels in the headbands stand out.

The masterpiece of twelfth-century Russian icon painting is the enormous icon *St. Nicholas* from the Novodevichi Monastery (plate 16). The saint, later worshiped in

68

35. Master of Novgorod
St. Joseph and the Prophetess Anna
(*detail of* Presentation of Christ in the Temple)
Copy of a 14th-century fresco from the Church of the Dormition of the Virgin, Volotovo

The Church of the Dormition of the Virgin, founded in 1352 and destroyed in 1941, was decorated with frescoes, the main themes of which were the anchorite way of life and the life of the Virgin. According to *The Chronicles of Novgorod,* which do not mention the name of the painter, the frescoes were executed in 1363. This date, however, probably refers to earlier frescoes, of which a few traces were visible. The technique, style, and colors used in the famous Volotovo frescoes indicate that the painter was familiar with the work of Theophanes the Greek, who began working in Novgorod in 1378. The Volotovo frescoes were executed in 1380. The Novgorod painter Russified Theophanes' manner; the faces were typically Russian. The frescoes had the sheer vitality of Theophanes' work but not its pathos.

To the right of the scene reproduced here, the aged Simeon is receiving the Child from the hands of the Virgin. Anna is bent over a scroll and reading a prophecy that was fulfilled. Next to her, St. Joseph is carrying a pair of turtledoves to the temple as a sacrifice: "As it is written in the law of the Lord, every male that openeth the womb shall be called holy to the Lord; And to offer a sacrifice according to that which is said in the law of the Lord, A pair of turtledoves, or two young pigeons" (Luke 2:23–24); and, in the same chapter: "And there was one Anna, a prophetess . . . And she was a widow of about fourscore and four years, which departed not from the temple, but served God with fastings and prayers night and day" (36–37). The painter followed the text of the Gospel closely.

Russia as patron of the poor and unfortunate, is portrayed here as a wise teacher. In comparison with this face, which has been transfigured by the artist's winged imagination, the finest Fayum portraits seem inferior; looking at it we might believe that the high forehead is a sign of wisdom, and that the jagged line of the brow signifies anger. And indeed, the saint is looking sternly at the worshiper, with a piercing glance—but he is not doing so angrily, rather with sympathy. Not until Modigliani will we find again so bold a transformation of the proportions of the human face. But this moral sublimity, this sense of human dignity, was accessible only to the Old Russian masters.

In the icon known as *The Ustyug Annunciation* (plate 20) the two figures seem to have

36. *Theophanes the Greek*
The Archangel Gabriel with the Sphere
Copy of a 14th-century fresco
from the Church of the Dormition of the Virgin, Volotovo

Everything in this painting of a fresco destroyed in 1941 (*see* plate 35) contributes to an impression of peace and harmony. The archangel Gabriel stands tall and stately in his amply flowing robes. The shape of the head and the enormous wings that frame it recall the middle angel in Theophanes' *Trinity* (plate 32).

just stepped down from the columns of some ancient temple. The mighty angel holds out his hand to Mary, who, wearing a dark-red mantle, is inclining her head ever so slightly toward him. On her breast the head of the Child is just barely visible—a materialization of the archangel's announcement of the imminent birth of Christ. But most remarkable in this icon is the archangel's inspired face, with its thin, aquiline nose, the clearly outlined small mouth, the golden locks of hair, big sorrowful eyes, and dark eyebrows. While giving Mary the joyous tidings of the Redeemer's birth, he yet cannot conceal from her that sufferings lie in store for her Son.

The icon known as *The Dormition*, from the Desiatinny Monastery in Novgorod, may be ascribed to the twelfth-century Novgorod school. Unlike later icons on the same subject, in which all the figures are united by a common impulse and subordinated to the nimbus surrounding Christ, here the figures are separated and appear on an empty gold ground. This produces a joyless impression of man's forlornness. The subdued brown tones contrast with the cold blues.

Two characteristic features of the Russian school are more clearly marked in two other works of the same period—*The Panagia Virgin* (plate 23) and *The Holy Face* (plate 18). The former comes from Yaroslavl, the latter possibly from Novgorod, but this is conjecture.

The Panagia Virgin was meant to serve in the place of a mural such as *The Indestructible Wall* at Kiev. The figure is a graceful, almost classical likeness of a woman

37. *School of Moscow:* The Virgin of the Don
Icon. 14th century, second half. Egg tempera on wood, 33⅞ x 26¾"
Tretyakov Gallery, Moscow

The Virgin of the Don is of the same type as the Virgin of Mercy and Gentleness, the origin of which can be traced to *The Virgin of Vladimir* (plate 6). The tender expression of the Child, however, is more lyrical. His little feet are resting on His Mother's hand. Mother and Child are looking in each other's eyes, and the way the Mother holds the Child is treated less hieratically.

According to tradition, this icon was a gift from the Don warriors to Prince Dmitri Ivanovich before the battle of Kulikovo (1380). The *Chronicles* mention this icon, which was in the Cathedral of the Dormition at Koloma until the late sixteenth century. It was then transferred to the Cathedral of the Annunciation in the Kremlin. After a victory over the Tatars in 1591, Tsar Fyodor Ivanovich built a monastery (now the Museum of Ancient Architecture) and named it after the icon.

rendered in all her human charm and stateliness. Similar proportions and drapery treated in this way, so that we feel the supple body under it, are found only in the Constantinople ivories and marble reliefs. The oval of Mary's face is regular, her nose is straight, the brows arch, and the pink mouth is exquisitely drawn. Like all ideal portraits, this one is marked by a certain coolness and impassivity.

This Virgin is not only a woman and a mother but also a goddess and protectress; she breathes unearthly grandeur, her hands raised in a ritual gesture of prayer. This type of image came to take the place of the image of the Great Goddess, whom the ancient Slavs had worshiped. Apparently, some remnant of the disk-shaped solar symbols from the older religion survived in the icon. At all events, the Virgin portrayed here has become a rigorously constructed symbol. The four circles at the top (two medallions with angels, the halo about Mary's head, and the medallion containing the Child) form an inverted pyramid that is echoed in Mary's raised hands. At the bottom, this pyramid is opposed by the horizontal lines of what she is standing on. In this way the living figures of woman and child are transformed into a sign sufficiently *sui generis* for the eye to recognize it easily even from a considerable distance. The statuesque figure of the Virgin herself

38. The Dormition of the Virgin
Icon. 14th century, second half
Egg tempera on wood, 33⅞ x 26¾"
Tretyakov Gallery, Moscow

This icon is painted on the back of *The Virgin of the Don* (plate 37). The pathos of this work, and the faces of the apostles with their white highlights, recall the art of Theophanes the Greek. On either side of the Virgin are six apostles, with St. Peter and St. Paul in the left and right foreground. Behind each group is a Father of the Church, book in hand. They are set against the background of the blue glory, at the center of which stands Jesus. He is holding out the soul of the Virgin, symbolized by a child in swaddling clothes. Above Christ's halo is a red cherub. The inscription reads: "Dormition of the Holy Virgin."

becomes as symbolic as the half-figure of the Child in the medallion. This is what distinguishes it from *The Ustyug Annunciation:* here are planted the seeds of the spirituality that will triumph in Rublev's art.

The icon *The Holy Face* renders a canonical type well known in twelfth-century painting (Laon, Nereditsa, Studenitsa). The figure portrayed is less that of a suffering man than that of a ruler, to judge from the severe facial expression. Yet there is no anger in it; the face is hieratically calm. We have here an anticipation of the merciful Christ as He will be portrayed by the masters of the fifteenth century. The ideal character of the icon is stressed by the fact that it does not include the kerchief, the so-called sudarium. The face is alert, the eyebrows slightly raised, the eyes wide open, the pupils turned slightly to the left, the corners of the mouth drooping a bit. But there is nothing tense in it: the dominating expression is one of serenity.

In keeping with this is the harmoniousness of the form. The circle of the halo takes on the function of the frame of a medallion. There is roundness in the face, too, especially in the golden strands of hair. The organic shape of the head comes close to being a perfect circle. Didactic and dogmatic elements are not obtrusive in this icon. This is rather the image of the desired, the striven for, the ideal. This figure brings to mind Rublev's *Redeemer* of Zvenigorod.

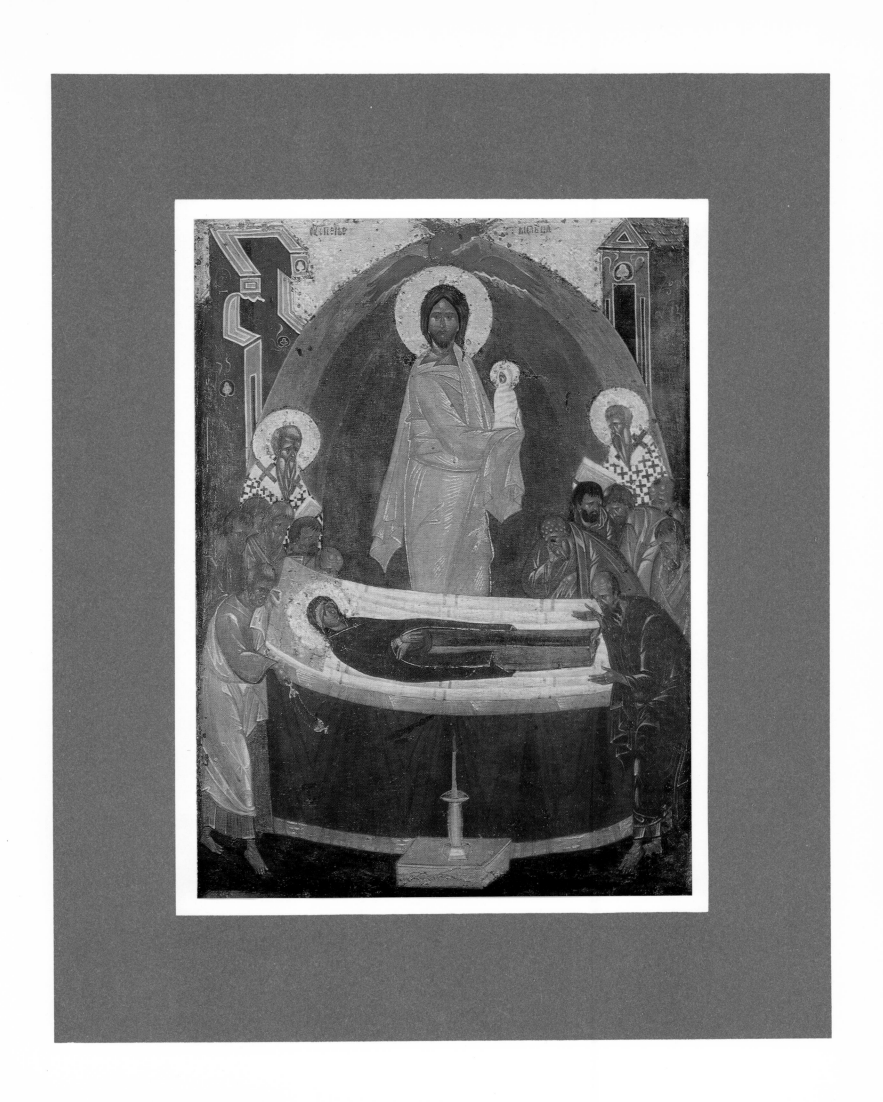

39. *School of Theophanes the Greek:* The Transfiguration
Icon. Early 15th century. Egg tempera on wood, 72½ x 52¾"
Tretyakov Gallery, Moscow

The Gospel account (Matt. 17:1–9) was faithfully followed by the great painter who executed this masterpiece. The symbolism is more explicit than that of Rublev's icon on the same subject (plate 43).

The disciples are prostrating themselves, overawed by Christ's blinding effulgence. St. Paul is kneeling at bottom left, with his hand in front of his eyes; St. John is in the middle; and St. James, hiding his face, is at the right. Left of center, Christ and His disciples are walking up Mount Tabor; right, after the miracle of the Transfiguration, they are walking down.

According to the Gospel account, Christ talked with the prophets Elias and Moses, and so we see them here. Nor has the painter forgotten the angels in the clouds who are showing the prophets the way.

The icon was originally in the Church of the Transfiguration at Pereslavl-Zalesky, which was a fief of the Muscovite princes from 1302 on. It was partly repainted in oil at the beginning of the twentieth century. Restored in 1924, it went to the Tretyakov Gallery in 1930.

A special place among these works is occupied by the *St. Demetrius of Salonika* from Dmitrov (plate 24). Here we have a resolute, angry, imperious warrior wearing the ducal crown, seated on his throne with half-drawn sword in hand. This celebration of the duke's power differs as greatly from other Russian icons as do the towers of a ducal castle from the domes of the churches.

Russian applied art of the time bears the same imprint of grandeur as the icons do. Novgorod tabernacles, and chalices made there by the masters Bratila and Kosta, are constructed clearly and rigorously. The tabernacles are models of a domed edifice with convex columns and doors with flat relief. In the chalices—or priests' communion cups—the figures are convex but the ornaments, derived from plant life, are flat. Russian annals of the time celebrate dukes who donated gold artifacts to churches for their embellishment. But in the silver objects from Novgorod the important thing is not the material but the clean shapes and beautiful proportions. The same is true of the four deësis figures on the vestments of Saint Varlaam of Khutyn, clearly silhouetted between small columns.

40. *School of Pskov:* The Virgin's Assembly
Icon. 14th century, second half. Egg tempera on wood, 31⅞ x 24"
Tretyakov Gallery, Moscow

There are several icons of the Virgin's Assembly. Each has its own iconography. Certain details of the Pskov icon remain hermetic, and one can only speculate on their meaning. In the upper part, around the Virgin, who sits enthroned, are (left) three angels without wings and (right) the shepherds. A little lower is the manger, with Christ in swaddling clothes. At the left of the Virgin's throne are the Magi, kneeling. The Virgin is holding a representation of the Christ Emmanuel inside a glory in the form of an eight-point star. The two tiny half-length figures on either side of the icon at the top are St. Nicholas and St. Barbara.

The icon comes from the Church of the Intercession of the Virgin at Pskov. Prior to this it was in the wooden church of St. Barbara.

Russian art prior to the Mongol invasion played an important part in the development of subsequent Russian art because it had roots in the humanistic culture of the Mediterranean. Not that the Russians slavishly imitated their Byzantine models—they mitigated the latters' austerity and asceticism and strove for a more harmonious form. The old cathedrals charm us by the grandeur embodied in them, and there is something of the same in the painting of the period. Although eleventh- and twelfth-century art is beautiful in itself, however, its grandeur stood in the way of its learning to express warm human feeling, as later Russian art would do.

The Mongol invasion early in the thirteenth century was a terrible blow to Russian culture. The Tatars overran Russia, ravaging it by their repeated incursions, and oppressed the population. The old links with Byzantium, the Balkans, and western Europe were broken. Important artistic projects became out of the question for a long time, stone edifices ceased to be built, and production of precious objects was halted. But artistic creation continued. Without understanding this period, it is hard to evaluate much that went on in Russia in later times.

Icons as old as the *St. Nicholas* from the Novodevichi Monastery (plate 16) had incorporated around the edges—on the same panel—small figures of an entirely different kind,

41. *School of Moscow:* The Feasts
Icon. Late 14th century. Egg tempera on wood, 12⅝ x 9⅞"
Tretyakov Gallery, Moscow

This small icon depicts on a single panel six scenes from the New Testament, each devoted to a feast of the church. It is an example of a type of icon known as Feasts. Reading from left to right, top to bottom: 1. The Annunciation. The crenelated wall symbolizes the Virgin's home. 2. The Nativity. Top left, wingless angels (old iconography); right, shepherds; center, the Virgin turned in the direction of the Magi; bottom left, St. Joseph; right, the Child's bath (this scene is very detailed). 3. The Transfiguration. 4. The Raising of Lazarus. Martha and Mary prostrate at Christ's feet. 5. The Descent to Limbo. Christ is holding out his hand to Adam, behind whom is Eve dressed in red. 6. The Ascension.

perhaps executed by apprentices. These figures are clumsy but full of character, their outlines clearly drawn, and brightly colored. They bear the imprint of folk art. Now, in this period of the barbarizing of art, we find more and more fresh, healthy energies making themselves felt. The Russian icons of this period bring to mind the Romanesque paintings of Catalonia.

In the icon *The Prophet Elijah* (plate 28), which is surrounded by episodes from his life, Elijah is pictured as a benign old man sitting on the ground. The forms have lost all gracefulness, seem hewn out of wood. To appreciate the suggestive force of the volumes out of which the folk artist has constructed his forms, we must compare this icon with such a work as the twelfth-century *Dormition*. Instead of subdued modulated tones the master employs pure bright colors. He decorates the icon's surface the same way Russian peasants were later to decorate their spinning wheels. He is particularly attracted by bright reds harmonizing with crimson and scarlet, contrasting with the cold tones of the old man's mantle and his blue-gray hair. We cannot say that the master of this icon was devoid of all painterly cultivation, but here folk taste breaks into painting. The episodes from the prophet's life are interesting in themselves, but they form a motley border around the figure of the prophet.

Andrey Rublev was working at Zvenigorod, near Moscow, in the early years of the fifteenth century. The Zvenigorod Monastery was founded by the monk Sava, a disciple of St. Sergey. (This monastery today is called Savino Storozhevsky.) The prince of Zvenigorod, Yuri, son of Dmitri Donskoy, was also the spiritual son of St. Sergey. Thus Rublev found himself in the spiritual climate of the environment in which he had grown up.

It is thought that Rublev painted a group of seven half-length figures for the monastery's Cathedral of the Nativity. However, only three of these, all of which are in the Tretyakov Gallery, are extant—those of St. Paul, the archangel Michael, and the Redeemer.

Rublev may have been familiar with the *chin* that had been brought to the Serpukhovs Monastery from Constantinople a short time before. However, he dealt with the theme in a very personal way, different from the austere stiffness of the Byzantines. St. Paul appears here as an angelic doctor, the wise author of the chapter on charity in the First Epistle to the Corinthians: "Though I speak with the tongues of men and of angels, and have not charity, I am become as sounding brass, or a tinkling cymbal" (I Corinthians 13:1).

The icon was found in 1918 in the Cathedral of the Dormition at Gorodok (Zvenigorod, near the Savino Storozhevsky Monastery).

Didacticism and asceticism have here disappeared from the icon, which has now become sheer pleasure to the eye.

On the Holy Gates of Tver, the faces of the Fathers of the Church are completely flat, the folds of their garments jagged, all the forms more clearly geometrized. In a later but still very archaic Novgorod icon, *Fatherland*, the faces of the Trinity and everything else heavenly have been given an extremely material, substantial, thinglike rendering. This violates the principle of a hierarchical order ascending from the terrestrial to the supraterrestrial, from the natural to the supernatural, which had been so typical of Byzantine art. The heavy throne is treated in the same way as the rocks in the *Elijah* icon.

The features of barbarization are most apparent in the applied arts. In 1359 the residents

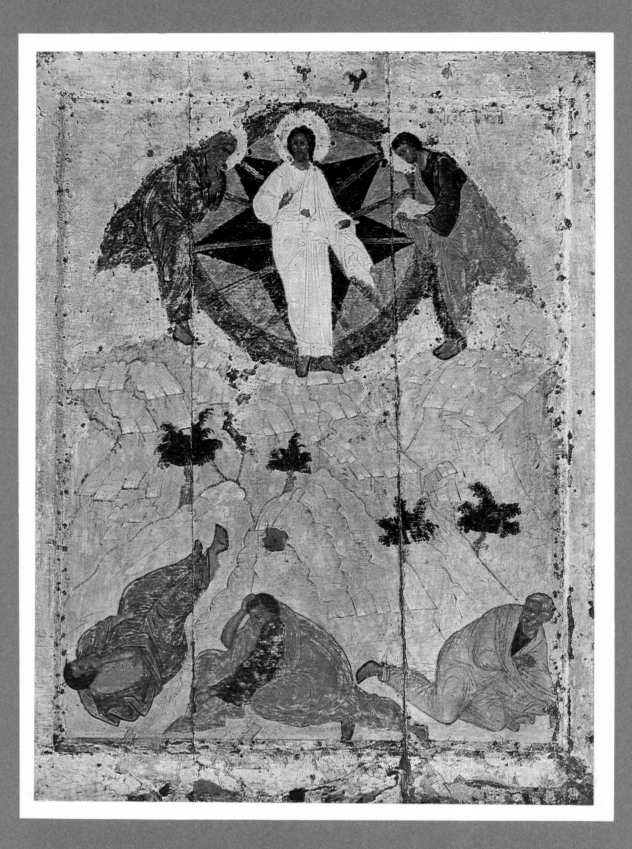

43. *Andrey Rublev (attributed)*
The Transfiguration
Icon. Early 15th century
Egg tempera on wood, 12¼ x 9⅞"
Cathedral of the Annunciation, Kremlin, Moscow

The Transfiguration is based on three passages of the Gospels. The following is from Matthew: "And after six days Jesus taketh Peter, James, and
John his brother, and bringeth them up into an high mountain apart,
and was transfigured before them: and his face did shine as the sun, and
his raiment was white as the light. And, behold, there appeared unto them
Moses and Elias talking with him" (Matt. 17:1–3).

   In keeping with tradition, the fear inspired by the miracle on Mount
Tabor is shown in the lower part of the icon. The disciples fall to the ground.
Peter, at lower right, starting to get up, raises his head, but in the dazzling light keeps his eyes down. The prophet Elias is at the upper left,
merging with the glory of Christ. Moses, on the right, is holding a scroll,
symbol of the Tables of the Law. The theme dates from the pre-Mongol era.

   The iconostasis of the Cathedral of the Annunciation in the Kremlin
was commissioned in 1405. The *Chronicles* mention the names of Theophanes the Greek, Rublev, and Prokhoros of Gorodetz. This *Transfiguration*
is attributed to Rublev on stylistic grounds.

44. St. Peter *(detail of plate 43)*

In 1408, Prince Vasily Dmitrievich commissioned Andrey Rublev and his older friend Danila Chorny to paint a series of frescoes. These were executed in the summer of that year. The Cathedral of the Dormition, built in the twelfth century, was to be redecorated.

Rublev's scenes from *The Last Judgment* are not frightening. They depict the beginning of the kingdom of the righteous in which there will be no room for hatred. The faces of the apostles, saints, and angels have an expression at once firm and gentle.

The face of St. Matthew, who is seated in the row of the apostles, is typically Russian. The suggestion of sadness in his expression is a characteristic of Rublev's work. Matthew is giving a blessing with his right hand; in his left he holds the open Gospel, on which his initials can be read. Behind him stand the angels.

of Liudgoshchinskaya Street in Novgorod, who were mostly craftsmen, built an immense carved wooden crucifix. Into it are set medallions, some representing folklore figures fighting dragons. St. George just barely manages to defeat an enormous dragon. Fyodor Tiron is saving a woman from a dragon, and Samson is making strenuous efforts to tear open the jaws of another dragon. The coiling tails of the animals end in volutes of the ornamentation that covers the surface of the crucifix. A similarly barbaric style can be found in small carved icons, such as the *St. George* in the Zagorsk Museum. Teratological motifs also appear in great abundance in illuminated books.

As it coarsened, art was impoverished. But this was a temporary state of affairs. Once liberated from the Tatars, the Russians renewed their ties with Byzantium, and there was a short but brilliant productive period under the Paleologues. By now they had accumulated enough experience and traditions of their own, so that the way was paved for Rublev.

The period from the end of the fourteenth to the beginning of the sixteenth century was

46. Christ *(detail of plate 47)*

47. *Andrey Rublev*
The Trinity
Icon. 1422–27
Egg tempera, 55⅞ x 44⅞"
Tretyakov Gallery, Moscow

The following statement appears in a seventeenth-century text: "The Most Venerated Andrey Radonezhsky, nicknamed Rublev, painted many holy icons, all of them magnificent. The same Andrey was a monk under the Venerated Father Nikon Radonezhsky. The latter, in his lifetime, asked him to paint the Most Holy Trinity in memory of Holy Father Sergey, the miracle worker."

The theme of Abraham's hospitality (Gen. 18:1–8) is here interpreted in a new way. The three hypostases of God appear as angels. In the center is Christ, with God the Father at the left and the Holy Ghost at the right. The theological theme is one of divine love, in which contemporaries also saw a prefiguration of the Last Supper. The only allusions to the Old Testament story are the oak of Mamre, where the encounter took place, and the small structure symbolizing Abraham's tent.

The work was discovered in 1904–1905. The heavy gold plate that concealed the entire painting except for the faces and hands was removed. In 1918–1919, the layers of paint added in the seventeenth and eighteenth centuries began to be removed. In 1926, however, it was decided to keep the late overpainting of the tree, because the original paint had disappeared.

From the Cathedral of the Trinity-St. Sergey Monastery in Zagorsk (near Moscow). On the iconostasis there, a copy of this work replaces the original.

This silk-thread embroidery showing a life-size image of St. Sergey of Radonezh was intended as a covering for a shrine with his relics, in the Cathedral of the Trinity in the monastery of which he was the abbot. According to the monastery tradition, this image of the saint is a portrait made about thirty years after his death (1392). The work was presented to the monastery in 1424 by the ruler of Moscow, Vasily I, son of Dmitri Donskoy.

It was probably commissioned in 1422, when St. Sergey was canonized and the cathedral built. In the same year, the abbot Nikon, who was a disciple of St. Sergey, commissioned Rublev to paint the icon *The Trinity*.

The embroidery was made in the workshop set up for Prince Vasily. Further light is thrown on the donation by the fact that his father had a special veneration for the saint, who sustained him in his struggle against the Tatars.

the most fruitful in all Russian art—a period of flowering not so much in architecture and monumental painting as in icon painting. This period stands out above all for Rublev's genius.

Russia was recovering from the Mongol invasions. Unified Russian forces successfully drove back the Tatars at Kulikovo in 1380. In the cultural domain, the city-state of Novgorod, which had not been ravaged by the Tatars, played a leading part. As Moscow gradually became the center of economic and political life, however, it now began to play an important cultural role. It was Moscow that colonized the north, and it was the rulers of Muscovy who were unifying the country. This paved the way for complete liberation from the Mongols at the close of the fifteenth century, under Ivan III. All these developments were supported by the people because they favored the country's economic, political, and cultural interests.

Now man begins to assume his right to address himself to God directly, without the intermediary of the Church. Although the Strigolnik heresy was crushed at Novgorod, it left traces. Of particular importance to culture was what was going on in the monasteries at this

The theme is that of Abraham's hospitality (Gen. 18:1–8), also called, in Russian iconography, "The Old Testament Trinity."

The angels are being served by Abraham, bearded, and Sarah, in red. The semicircular composition is dominated in the center by a tree symbolizing the oak of Mamre and by the small structure that represents Abraham's tent. The following is part of the text from Genesis interpreted by the painter: "And the Lord appeared unto him in the plains of Mamre: and he sat in the tent door in the heat of the day; And he lift up his eyes and looked, and, lo, three men stood by him: . . . And Abraham hastened into the tent unto Sarah, and said, Make ready quickly three measures of fine meal, knead it, and make cakes upon the hearth." The painter depicts here the very moment after the encounter. On the table are several dishes corresponding to the Biblical description. The clear, bright colors give an impression of warmth.

The icon was recently found in the Church of the Holy Ghost, in the Trinity-St. Sergey Monastery.

time, especially in the Trinity-St. Sergey Monastery. Although the Russian monasteries followed the rules laid down by the monasteries in Greece, they took part in secular life. They held their property in common, and labored for the good of the community. Sergey's conception of the earthly world is more than a little reminiscent of St. Francis'. Toward the end of the fifteenth century, heresy flared up again at Novgorod and later in Moscow (the Judaizing sect). Sporadic attempts were made to throw off the shackles of dogma, but the autocracy repressed free thought, the Church became the bastion of autocracy, and in it dogmatism and traditionalism became ever stronger.

In the fifteenth century, icon painting especially flourished and gained maturity. Great masters made their appearance, and local schools developed. Art preserved its ecclesiastical character, but everything that was stirring the people at the time was reflected in it. It came closer to man, giving expression to his feelings and preoccupations, and departed from tradition more often as it groped for new paths. Old Testament austerity gave way to greater warmth and tenderness in the spirit of the New Testament. Art was not so much dogmatic

The Crucifixion is a fragment of an embroidered cloth on which the feasts of the Trinity are also represented. This embroidery was commissioned by the wife of a Novgorod boyar and executed in the prince's workshop in Moscow. The artists were foreigners, probably of Serbian origin.

as philosophical. The icon became not so much an object of worship as of contemplation, through which the eternal mysteries of existence are revealed to man. Now art gives man a keener sense of his nearness to heavenly felicity. Instead of crushing him with its grandeur, or terrifying him, it caresses his eye, stimulates his imagination, arouses humane feeling in him, and brings joy into his life.

Russian painting became a high art. Even toward the close of the fifteenth century, when solemn, grandiose elements became stronger as art more and more reflected the court-centered tastes of Moscow, there was no official coldness in it.

The most important event in the artistic life of the second half of the fourteenth century was the arrival in Moscow of the great Byzantine master Theophanes (plates 32–34, 36), who had already worked for a time in Novgorod. Theophanes brought to Russia not only the achievements of the Paleologue school but his own incomparably brilliant mastery. He was fully appreciated in Russia.

In his decorations for the Church of the Transfiguration of the Redeemer in Novgorod (1378) (plates 32–34), his paintings of old men are the most impressive. On the drum of the cupola it is the patriarchs who stand out, in the choirs the hermits—especially the figure of the aged *St. Macarius* (plate 34). In these figures Theophanes reveals a depth of experience such as art had scarcely known before him. They express the call to contemplation that the Hesychasts had launched, but also inner conflicts, man's struggle with himself. Theophanes' old men have been through a great deal. They pray, but prayer brings no relief; they shun worldly temptation, but do not attain peace of mind thereby.

Theophanes attained perfect mastery of the technique of mural painting. He does not wield his brush as evenly as had been usual before him, but makes discontinuous strokes and paints harsh lights. In all his creations we sense the movements of his hand holding the brush. He used a subdued scale of warm incarnadine tones with harsh lights thrown on top of them. Even today the colors painted by his brilliant hand give the impression that they are not yet quite dry. In Moscow, Theophanes executed the main icons of the deësis tier in the Cathedral of the Annunciation (1405), a series of controlled, majestic, strongly characterized figures. Mary in her dark blue cloak stretches out her arms toward Christ, and John bows before him in an olive and gold cloak.

Theophanes introduced dramatic passion into Russian art, and especially enriched painting with the techniques of modeling and chiaroscuro. All the Novgorod and Moscow masters were influenced by him, but this did not prevent them from searching out their own ways.

The most original painting of the Novgorod school in this period that survived into the twentieth century was the decoration of the Church of the Dormition of the Virgin on the Volotovo Field outside Novgorod. The Nazis razed it to the ground, and its marvelous paintings were destroyed. Theophanes preferred balanced compositions (such as *The Trinity*, plate 32), but the world of the Volotovo frescoes was filled with movement and earthly passions, the human figures deeply stirred by the revelation of Godhead. The earthly life of Christ and Mary was treated with the greatest care.

The *Archangel Gabriel with the Sphere* (plate 36) at Volotovo was a good example of Theophanes' art. This angel is not as solemn and severe as the Byzantine angels. He is a tall, bony youth. His enormous wings give him grandeur, and the jagged folds of the drapery give the figure movement. The mural is painted in broad, gentle strokes. Raspberry reds, lilacs, pinks, and olive greens predominate. Warm and cold tones form a modulated chromatic harmony. The mirror in the angel's hand reflects a blue sky with white clouds and a pink earth with yellow rocks.

The art of the fourteenth-century Novgorod murals was echoed in icons made there in the same period, particularly the icon of the archangel Gabriel, which formed part of the deësis, and one of the *Nativity* with clearly drawn pink hills and blue highlights.

At the turn of the fourteenth–fifteenth centuries, Moscow became the most important artistic center in the Grand Duchy of Muscovy. A new type of church was developed, one outstanding example of which is the recently restored cathedral of the Andronikov Monastery. The Moscow masters succeeded in combining the rectangular body of the edifice with the domes, utilizing for the latter the form of a female coiffure in three tiers, the *kokoshnik*. There is reason to believe that the masons here followed models of folk architecture in wood. Architecture became more dynamic, more spiritualized.

A significant event in Russian art during this period was the creation of the iconostasis. The earliest known iconostasis was executed in 1405 in the Cathedral of the Annunciation by Theophanes, Prokhoros, and Rublev (plate 43). Many years of artistic experimentation are embodied in it. From that time on, every Russian church had its iconostasis.

Embroidery in gold and silver thread, realistic in style, represents the scene of lamentation around the body of the dead Christ. In iconography and style this work is close to a mid-fifteenth-century *Threnody* executed for the Cathedral of Hagia Sophia in Novgorod. Moscow and Novgorod were the two great embroidery centers. The present work came from the Kirillovo-Belozersky Monastery.

An iconostasis consists of several tiers of icons forming a sort of wall between the sanctuary or altar space and the main body of the church. It is something like the *jubé* or rood loft in the Gothic cathedral and at the same time like the polyptych in Italian churches.

The iconostasis was not a product of abstract theological thought but of popular art; it met the need of portraying the saints as champions of mankind before the throne of God. This profoundly humane idea found its most grandiose and harmonious expression by placing on both sides of the icon of Christ a series of icons showing Mary, John the Baptist, the archangels, the apostles, and the Fathers of the Church. All are represented with arms outstretched, supplicating God to show mercy to mortal men and women "here below."

Whereas in the Hagia Sophia at Kiev the mosaic figures are arranged hierarchically (plates 8–12), in the iconostasis they are arranged in tiers, all at the same height, according to the classical principle of isocephalism. What is new here is that subjection of man to the rule of a severe God has given way to union of man with God through spiritual fervor, the human hope for mercy and forgiveness clearly expressed in the attitudes and glances the figures direct at Christ.

The Ghent altarpiece by the Van Eycks obliges the viewer to get close to it and study its meticulously painted details. The Russian iconostasis is calculated to be seen from afar by a large gathering of the devout. To be sure, under these circumstances details are indistinguishable, but the general relations among the figures stand out clearly. What

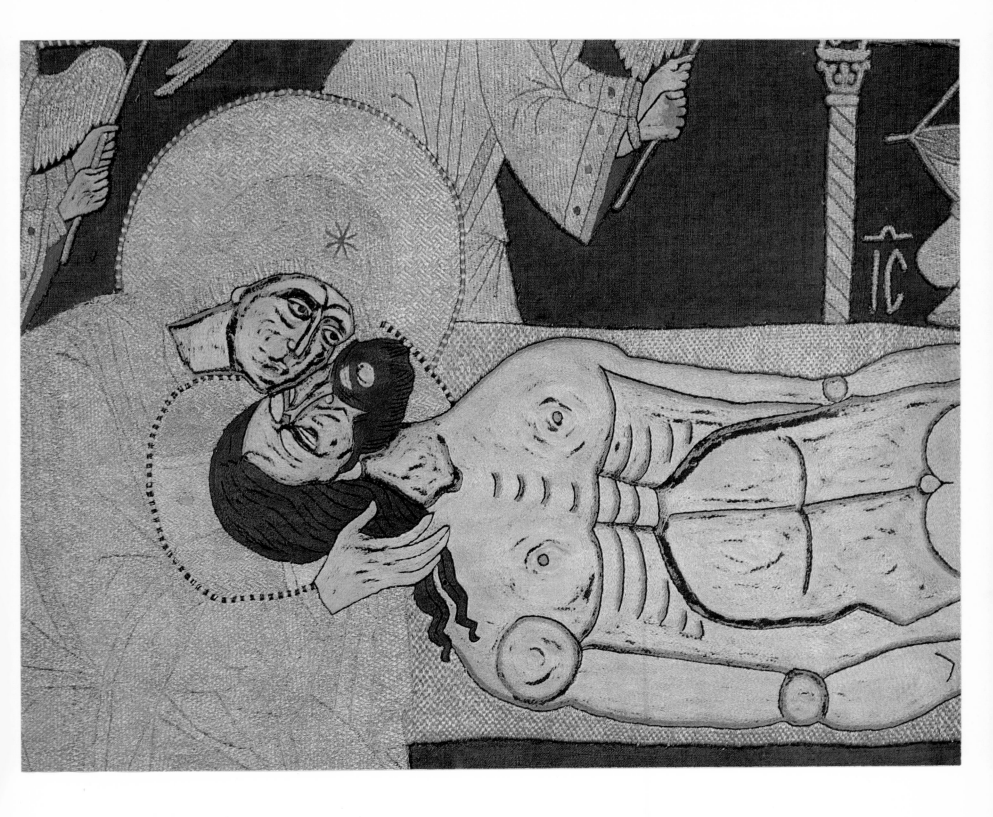

The *St. George* icon, also known as "St. George and the Miracle of the Dragon," illustrates a legend of the Greek East going back to pre-Christian beliefs. St. George is overpowering the terrible beast, which fed on human flesh, and thereby saves the life of a young princess.

There are two variants of this theme in Russian iconography. In one of these, the holy warrior's victory is witnessed by the princess, king, queen, and people. In the other, the story is reduced to a symbol whose expressive power lies in its terseness, a quality characteristic of the masterpieces of Russian art.

All we are shown here is St. George plunging his lance into the dragon's mouth. At top right, God's hand appears in the clouds, blessing the saint. Above the horse's head, to St. George's left, is a shield on which the sun is represented as a face emitting rays.

The cult of St. George in Russia dates from the pre-Mongol period. It replaced both the sun worship of the pagan Slavs and the cult of the fertility god Yaril. This may be why the sun is represented on the saint's shield.

dominates is the principle of group participation characteristic of folk art. The viewer joins, so to speak, in a procession moving toward the center.

The iconostasis played an important role in the development of Russian painting. It compelled the masters to look upon every icon as an element of a complex whole, and thereby helped strengthen compositional structure, which now became an indispensable feature of every Russian icon. Intended to be seen from a considerable distance, the icons had to possess great generality in their forms. Clarity of silhouette became a hallmark of Russian icon painting in the fifteenth century. The deësis figures are in fact easily recognizable by their characteristic attributes: the Fathers of the Church by the crosses on their chasubles, John the Baptist by his ascetically thin bare legs, and so on.

Many icons, particularly those on the subjects "All living things rejoice in Thee" and the Intercession of the Virgin, are—so to speak—iconostases in miniature.

Good examples of the Moscow school of icon painting in the fourteenth century are such

55. The Entombment
Icon. Late 15th century
Egg tempera on wood, 35⅞ x 24¾"
Tretyakov Gallery, Moscow

The Virgin, John the Divine, and Joseph of Arimathea are bidding farewell to Christ. Mary Magdalene, dressed in red in accordance with the iconographic tradition, is standing with arms upraised. Nicodemus is standing at the right.

This icon was part of an iconostasis that included *The Descent from the Cross* (now in the Tretyakov Gallery) and *The Last Supper* (in the Museum of Russian Art, Kiev). It was acquired in Gorodetz, a town on the Volga, but there is reason to think that it may have come from Kargopolis.

icons as *The Tolgsk Virgin* (which came from Yaroslavl, plate 29) showing Mary enthroned as in Italian works of the *duecento*, with its warm saturated colors, and *SS. Boris and Gleb on Horseback* (plate 30), with the two beautifully drawn silhouettes of the horses. Dating from the second half of that century are icons like *The Virgin of the Don* (plate 37), in which Mary has a more living expression than *The Virgin of Vladimir* (plate 6) as she inclines her head toward the Child. On the back of *The Virgin of the Don* is a representation of the Dormition, the pathos of which brings to mind Theophanes. The miniature icon *The Feasts* (late fourteenth century, plate 41) has tender blues and a softness of execution that anticipate Rublev.

Nonetheless, when we finally come to Rublev's own works, after looking at those of all his predecessors, we are filled with amazement and admiration, feel ourselves to be in the presence of a miracle of art, wisdom, simplicity, perfection, and vitality. The fascination of this art is irresistible. There is a feminine tenderness in it, but also strength and solidity; besides grandeur there is captivating suavity, spiritual purity, and restraint. How great were the spiritual riches of a people that, having so lately survived national tragedy, succeeded in revealing to the world its luminous poetic dream through the creations of this great artist!

Rublev painted some of the Feasts in the iconostasis of the Cathedral of the Annunciation (which dates from 1405). In these works Theophanes' tense, dramatic quality

Though following the Gospel closely, the painter has combined two themes, the Women at the Tomb (two of them are carrying vials of aromatics) and Christ Appearing to the Holy Women.

The women are amazed at finding the tomb empty of all save the shroud. An angel in white is telling them of the Resurrection. The Gospel description has been followed to the letter: ". . . and seeth the linen clothes lie, And the napkin, that was about his head, not lying with the linen clothes, but wrapped together in a place by itself" (John 20:6–7).

In the same icon we see the risen Christ. The position of his hand is based on the text "Touch me not: for I am not yet ascended to my Father" (John 20:17).

The icon comes from St. Nicholas' Church in the village of Gostinopolya, in the Novgorod area.

gives way to harmonious clarity. The icon *The Transfiguration* (plate 43), like that on

the same subject from the Pereslavl school influenced by Theophanes (plate 39), portrays the

terror of the apostles, who have thrown themselves to the ground, and the visions of the

prophets on either side of the radiant Christ. But in Rublev, instead of dramatic tension,

instead of emphasis upon the apostles' bewilderment, we find a joyous, festive mood in which

individual thoughts and feelings are dissolved. The figure of Christ in His white robe, the main

source of light, is easily inscribed in a circle; the outlines of the prophets bowing before

Christ coincide with the upper part of the circle, and together the three figures form

a beautiful rosette. The prostrate apostles are separated from the prophets by transparent

hills with sparsely scattered bushes. Rublev renounces Theophanes' strong contrasts between

light and shadow; his icon is flooded with light, seems to radiate light. The clear-cut

silhouettes of the figures serve only to enhance the impression of light. These features of

The Transfiguration will eventually become characteristic of all icons of the Moscow school.

In 1408, Andrey Rublev and his older friend Danila Chorny were commissioned to

decorate the old Cathedral of the Dormition at Vladimir. Rublev was of course familiar with

57. Church of the Holy Ghost. *1476*
Trinity-St. Sergey Monastery, Zagorsk

The church was built by Pskov architects on the
site of a former wooden Church of the Trinity. The
architects who had worked on the Moscow Kremlin
for Ivan the Great were invited to design this structure.

During the Lithuanian and Polish invasion of
1608–1610, this small church figured in the Russian
defense, its bell sounding the alarm. The building is
one of the oldest belfry churches in Russia. Many
buildings were added to the church over the centuries, but its original purity was restored between
1939 and 1949.

58. Cathedral of the Annunciation. *1484–89*
Kremlin, Moscow

Smaller than the Cathedral of the Dormition in the
Kremlin, the cathedral shown here was the pala-
tine chapel, connected by galleries with the prince's
palace. It was probably built by architects from
Pskov.

Originally it had three domes. Galleries and further domes were added in the sixteenth century.

the mural *The Last Judgment* in the Cathedral of St. Dmitri in Vladimir, which had been executed by an excellent Greek master toward the end of the twelfth century. The Russian master was now to create his own version of the traditional subject (plate 45). To the idea of dreadful punishments inflicted on man for his misdeeds, man's consciousness of his insignificance and sinfulness, Rublev opposes man's luminous hope in the mercy of God, the joyous aspiration of the righteous to eternal bliss, and his own fascination with man's earthly, visible beauty, including the charm of youth.

59. *Dionysius*
Metropolitan Alexey
Icon. Late 15th or early 16th century
Egg tempera on wood, 77⅝ x 59⅞″
Tretyakov Gallery, Moscow

Metropolitan Alexey (c. 1295–1378) is standing in the middle, full face, against a pale green background with light clouds. His right hand is raised in blessing, and he holds a Gospel in his left. His vestments are embroidered with gilded crosses and geometric ornamentation. In color and decoration, the vestments closely resemble the metropolitan's robe preserved in the Museum of the Palace of Arms at the Moscow Kremlin.

The hagiographic scenes around the border read from left to right, top to bottom, disregarding the central panel. The first five scenes (top border) relate the birth and vocation of young Eleutherius, a boyar's son who became a monk, under the name of Alexey, and, later, bishop of Vladimir.

Certain of the scenes allude to historical facts in the life of the great prelate. He was appointed regent of the young Prince Dmitri Ivanovich (named Donskoy after the battle of Kulikovo, which was fought near the banks of the Don River) and governed wisely until the prince came of age.

Three scenes deal with the metropolitan's delicate mission to the lands of the Tatar khan. In scene 9 (left border, third from top) he is shown before his departure, venerating the relics of his predecessor, Metropolitan Pyotr; in the background we make out, behind the tomb, the Cathedral of the Dormition in the Moscow Kremlin, where the relics were preserved. In scene 10 (right border, third from top) the khan, impressed by the great prelate's dignity and wisdom, is kneeling before him. In scene 11 (directly under scene 9) the metropolitan is healing the khan's wife, shown reclining in bed. Oddly, one of the saint's meetings with the khan is placed in the upper right-hand corner (scene 6). The khan, seated and surrounded by his bodyguards, is presenting the metropolitan with a richly worked piece of furniture. Standing behind the metropolitan are boyars who are bringing the khan gifts of gilt brocade. Opposite the scene of the healing of the khan's wife is scene 12, showing the metropolitan's welcome back to Moscow; he is being greeted by Prince Ivan Ivanovich, Dmitri's father, whom he is blessing. Behind the prince's retinue we see the crenelated walls of Moscow. The architecture symbolizes the prince's palace and the Cathedral of the Dormition.

Three scenes deal with the meeting between the Metropolitan Alexey and the abbot of the Trinity-St. Sergey Monastery. The latter, Sergey of Radonezh, is accompanied by his disciple, the monk Andronik. Just under scene 1, which represents the birth of Eleutherius, Sergey of Radonezh, in the company of two monks, presents himself to the seated metropolitan. The latter asks Sergey to appoint Andronik abbot of the Monastery of the Holy Redeemer, which had been founded by the metropolitan in 1361. (This monastery was later called the Andronikov Monastery and is today the Icon Museum in Moscow.) In scene 8 the metropolitan is blessing Andronik in his new function; in the background is the Monastery of the Redeemer, with an image of the Holy Face. The third of these scenes

(continued on page 114)

(continued from page 112)

(scene 13; plate 60) shows the metropolitan, who, feeling that his end is near, asks Sergey to replace him as metropolitan of Moscow. The scene opposite this shows Alexey looking on and speaking to the masons, who are building his tomb; behind them rises the Monastery of the Miracle of the Archangel Michael in the Kremlin.

The bottom row of scenes depicts the discovery of the saint's relics, his miracles, and his death.

Scene 15 (bottom left corner) shows his burial. It is followed by the discovery of his relics and the raising of a child from the dead. The last scene shows the miraculous healing of Naum, a crippled monk. These scenes take place in the Monastery of the Miracle of the Archangel Michael, which is seen in the background.

Some of the scenes deal with historical facts confirmed by chronicles: the episcopate of 1352, the appointment as metropolitan, the journey to the khan in 1357. The chronicles also mention the miraculous healing of the monk Naum. Moreover, Archbishop Gennady of Moscow built a church in the saint's honor; the latter's relics were transferred to it in 1483.

It is assumed that Dionysius made use of the saint's life that had been written in 1486.

The icon comes from the Cathedral of the Dormition in the Moscow Kremlin.

60. SS. Sergey and Alexey *(detail of plate 59)*

The exquisite figures of the trumpet-blowing angels hovering in mid-air are not at all threatening—they are smiling. The torments of the sinner are all but ignored. Rublev focused his attention on the figures of the people being admitted to paradise in expectation of heavenly bliss. The Fathers of the Church had taught that "Man must turn away from external beauty, avert his eyes that at every waking moment seek to look upon corporeal beauty and splendor, and meditate on death." Rublev found in himself the strength to overcome such medieval asceticism. The faces of his pensive angels and the figures of the apostles on both sides of the Almighty are pervaded with a richness of spiritual life that Old Russian art had never known. These figures also disclose Rublev's characteristic manner, the peculiarities of his pictorial form. He rejects the harsh, angular highlights of Theophanes the Greek. The figures are traced in flowing, rounded contours, the lights are painted gently, and this is why the bodies, though not entirely flat, are extremely light, almost airy.

61. *Dionysius*
The Crucifixion
Icon. 1500
Egg tempera on wood, 33½ x 20½"
Tretyakov Gallery, Moscow

By elongating his figures, Dionysius stresses their symbolic meaning. There are groups at either side of the Cross. In the left foreground are the Virgin, Mary Magdalene, Mary of Cleophas, and Mary, mother of James. The Virgin is being held up by Mary Magdalene. In the group at the right are St. John, who is leaning forward with his hand on his chest, and, slightly behind and in contrast with him, Longinus the centurion, holding a shield.

Above the crenelated wall representing Jerusalem are two pairs of angels, one symbolizing the coming of the church of the New Testament, and the other the departure of the synagogue, the church of the Old Testament. Above the Crucifixion are two lamenting angels.

The work was created for the iconostasis in the Cathedral of the Trinity at St. Paul's Monastery near Vologda. On the back of an icon entitled *The Redeemer in Glory,* from the same iconostasis, is the transcription of an older inscription, traces of which are visible a little higher: "The deësis, the feasts, and the prophets were painted by Dionysius in 1500." The older text may have been inscribed by the painter himself.

Thanks to the predominantly generalized regular contours, the frescoes harmonize with the architectural features of the church, its vaults, arches, and soaring pillars. Rublev's frescoes do not clutter the walls but blend easily with the architectural space.

A work wholly of Rublev's creation is the so-called *Zvenigorod Chin* (a range of saints and Church Fathers approaching a central deësis), three figures from which have come down to us—the Redeemer, the archangel Michael, and St. Paul (plate 42). These figures captivate us with their rare combination of gracefulness and strength, softness and firmness, but most of all by their boundless goodness of heart. It is enough to recall earlier works such as *The Holy Face,* dating from the twelfth century, or *The Archangel Michael* (plate 52), from the fourteenth, to realize that with Rublev we have entered the century when moral ideas and ideals centered on humanity. The Zvenigorod *Redeemer,* with His harmonious face, open, frank expression, is looking kindly upon mankind. This divinity is not so much omnipotent as beautiful—like *Le Beau Dieu,* the well-known statue at Amiens.

62 and 63. *Dionysius and his sons Theodosius and Vladimir*
Holy Warriors
Fresco. 1500–1502
Therapont Monastery, Church of the Nativity of the Virgin

The monumental style of these figures is in marked contrast to the refined elongation of the figures in the *Intercession of the Virgin* (plate 65). But here, too, the hands and heads are small. The style of the work and the postures recall the figures of St. George and St. Demetrius painted by Theodosius in 1508 on one of the pillars of the Cathedral of the Annunciation in the Moscow Kremlin.

The most striking characteristic of these frescoes is the richness of the half tones, which are extraordinarily luminous. Unfortunately, some of them have been painted over and have lost their original brilliance.

64. *Theodosius, son of Dionysius*
The Last Judgment
Fresco. 1508
Cathedral of the Annunciation, Kremlin, Moscow

This fresco is composed of several scenes. As in Rublev's fresco *The Last Judgment* in Vladimir, the joyousness of the Elect is the most prominent feature. In style this work is very similar to the Therapont frescoes (plate 65).

65. *Dionysius and his sons Theodosius and Vladimir*
Intercession of the Virgin
Fresco. 1500–1502
Therapont Monastery, Church of the Nativity of the Virgin

The Therapont Monastery is on the shores of a northern lake not far from the Kirillovo-Belozersky Monastery. It was founded in the fourteenth century by a disciple of St. Cyril of Belozersk. In the fifteenth century it became a great intellectual and spiritual center. Many prominent Muscovites retired to it in their old age.

One of the most important groups of frescoes that have been preserved, these cover the walls of the monastery's cathedral from dome to floor.

The scene of the Intercession, situated in a lunette, is one of a group of three. The two other themes are the Glorification of the Virgin and "Every breath glorifies thee."

The iconography of the Intercession is Byzantine and goes back to the tenth century. As presented here, the scene takes the form that was developed in the fourteenth and fifteenth centuries on the basis of the Rostov-Suzdal and, later, Moscow versions.

In the Therapont fresco the Virgin is standing and holding a veil. Behind her is the church. She is surrounded by angels and saints. In the right foreground, among the saints, St. Andrey is pointing out the apparition of the Virgin to his disciple Epiphanius. At the left, in a pulpit, St. Romanus the Melodist is holding a scroll: he was the author of many hymns to the Virgin. Behind him are singers and monks.

The angels appear as protectors of mankind. In the work of the Master of the Kremlin they symbolize the archangels Michael, Gabriel, Raphael, and Uriel.

Here, too, the painter interprets the text from Revelation in his own way: "Loose the four angels which are bound in the great river Euphrates. And the four angels were loosed, which were prepared for an hour, and a day, and a month, and a year, for to slay the third part of men" (Rev. 9:14–15).

The icon of *St. Paul* is majestically serene. This sage, with his high forehead, is not so much turning to Christ in supplication as following his own train of thought. The softly flowing folds of his cloak emphasize the harmoniousness of his face. The Zvenigorod icons disclose Rublev's rare gifts as a colorist. Such pure sonority of colors, such subtlety of shadings and half tones, had been unknown in previous Russian and even in Byzantine icon painting. The colors have a radiance that was alien to Theophanes. Rublev's chromatic qualities are in keeping with the softness and tenderness that pervade his faces.

Rublev's *Trinity* (plate 47) is the best known of all Russian icons. It truly sums up the finest features of the Russian school. In Byzantine Trinities the "historical, literal meaning" holds sway: the Byzantine artists always portrayed Abraham and Sarah serving the three angels. In Rublev, the "prophetic meaning" predominates. Abraham and Sarah are omitted, and the three angels are conversing about the mystery of the Incarnation. This icon transports us to the empyrean. In Byzantine icons treating the same subject, and particularly in Theophanes' (plate 32), the middle angel dominates the two others, who bow to him, and the picture may be interpreted as showing God with two companions. In Rublev's work all three angels are bowing their heads to one another. Love, friendship, and

67. *Master of the Kremlin*
Rider on the Black Horse (*detail of* The Apocalypse)
Icon. Late 15th century
Egg tempera on wood
Cathedral of the Dormition, Kremlin, Moscow

The huge icon *The Apocalypse,* two details of which are reproduced here, was attributed until recently to Dionysius. It is the work of a member of his school, whose name has not come down to us. Although there are borrowings from Dionysius' style, notably in the marked elongation of the figures, and though the work is deeply influenced by Rublev's harmonious sense of color, it has an individuality all its own. It embodies a new humanism, which is expressed with a vigor and emotional tension contrasting alike with Rublev's serenity and Dionysius' solemn restraint.

unity—this is the "moral meaning" of Rublev's icon. Not for nothing was it painted in memory of St. Sergey, who bade his disciples live in amity. Moreover, the icon has "symbolic meaning." The angels also stood for the three persons of the Trinity, the chalice symbolizes the chalice of death, the tree the Tree of Life, the mountain symbolizes "the sublime," etc. The whole icon seems to be composed of hieroglyphs capable of raising man from the realm of sense perception to that of intellectual perception. At the same time, it charms the modern viewer unfamiliar with theological subtleties. It has something about it akin to the scenes on Attic tombs of the fifth century B.C., showing the deceased saying farewell to his family. The icon arouses not only reverence as a sacred object but also admiration as a masterpiece of art. Its aesthetic qualities are not overshadowed by its theological profundity. The viewer senses something sublime behind all life, and this fills him with reverence for earthly things. An endless world of meanings opens up to him. Looking at the figures of three winged youths, he divines, so to speak, the mystery of the universe. He is filled with confidence in nature and a sense of extraordinary freedom.

The three figures in the icon compose a group easily inscribable within a circle. In the lower part of the icon the elements of a hexahedron can be discerned. The circle usually symbolizes heaven, God, eternity. But in Rublev's icon it does not produce the impression

68. *School of Moscow:* St. John the Divine on Patmos
Icon. Early 16th century. Egg tempera on wood, 36⅝ x 28″
Tretyakov Gallery, Moscow

In the center of this hagiographic icon is St. John, who is looking up. Prochorus is seated opposite him, writing. Iconographically, the scene derives from the model created at the end of the fourteenth century by Andrey Rublev in the Khotrovo Gospel miniature on the same subject.

Scenes from the life of St. John are depicted around the border. The upper and lower bands read from left to right. The six other scenes alternate back and forth across the picture.

Upper border: 1. The apostles drawing lots at Gethsemane. 2. St. John and Prochorus caught in a storm at sea. 3. Prochorus helping St. John disembark at Ephesus after the storm. 4–5. St. John and Prochorus preaching in the baths. 6. (*directly below scene 5*) A supliant begging St. John to heal his son. 7. (*below scene 1*) Raising the suppliant's son, who had been choked by a devil in the bath. 8. (*below scene 7*) Baptizing the Ephesians. 9. (*below scene 6*) St. John preaching against followers of the cult of Dionysius. 10. (*below scene 9*) Curing of the man possessed by a devil. 11. (*under scene 8*) Christ appearing to St. John.

Lower border: 12. Healing of the burned man. 13. Exorcism. 14. Healing of the leper. 15. St. John giving the Evangelists the book dictated to Prochorus. 16. Dormition of St. John.

of something thought up in advance, something added to the picture. The circle seems produced of itself, just as the three figures incline their heads toward one another, the two lateral figures before the middle one. The circle is a static element, yet it does not exclude movement. In the upper part, the symmetry is disturbed by the inclination of the middle angel's head; in the lower part, the balance is restored by the slight rightward displacement of the seats. The composition of *The Trinity* allows for different readings: it may seem to evoke a *tondo*, but at the same time the figures form a sort of bouquet with stems tied together at the bottom. A pyramidal pattern may also be detected in the icon. The space between the angels' legs is shaped somewhat like a chalice, and this chalice echoes the shape of the middle angel.

The space in the icon similarly allows for different readings: the three figures are arranged so that they do not overlap, and hence it might be supposed that all are in the same

69. Cathedral of the Archangel Michael. *1505–9*
Kremlin, Moscow

70. Ivan Veliky Bell Tower. *1505–1600*
Kremlin, Moscow

On the whole, the general plan of this five-domed church was inspired by the traditional layout of Moscow churches, but the exterior decoration recalls fifteenth-century Italian architecture: classical pilasters, capitals, and soffits here make their first appearance in Russia. The princes of Moscow, and later the Tsars, were buried in this cathedral.

This structure was the last monument built in the middle of the Kremlin, where it towered above the domes of the other buildings. Around it are churches that, though designed by different architects, give an impression of unity. Work on the highest dome was not completed until 1600.

plane, as in a relief. At the same time, the middle figure is situated on the second or even the third plane (the angels on each side are on the first, the table on the second), and thus the composition looks concave. But since the middle angel is larger than the angels on each side and painted more compactly, it comes forward, and the whole group may also be perceived as convex.

71. St. George. *15th century*
Polychrome wood sculpture, 47⅞ x 29⅛ x 6¾″
Yuriev-Polski Museum, vicinity of Vladimir

The Holy Warrior is wearing a coat of mail. A red cloak is thrown over his shoulder. His horse is rearing. The face and entire figure of the saint resemble those of a polychrome stone sculpture of the same subject that was executed in 1464 by V. Ermolin for one of the towers of the Moscow Kremlin. Ermolin, who was also an architect, was sent to Yuriev-Polski in 1471 to restore the Cathedral of St. George.

Sculpture never greatly developed in Russia because the church interiors were decorated with icons, frescoes, and mosaics. Some churches had bas-reliefs on the outside, but this was quite unusual. Sculpture was a folk art and did not become a fine art until the classical period.

The present work is made of lime wood and is painted in tempera.

Rublev's contours render the organic structure of flexible, harmonious figures. The icon subtly renders the organic beauty of the human body—particularly beautiful is the hand of the angel at the right. At the same time, down to the smallest details of the hands, the outlines of the figures are part of the rhythm of fluid rounded lines, a rhythm that generates the circular composition of the icon as a whole. Only the building in the background and the vertical drapery are opposed to the organicity of the bodies, and they strengthen the architecture of the whole.

Similar uniformities can be detected in the coloring. The figures are more compact chromatically than the objects in the distance. The drooping sleeve of the middle angel is heavier than the blue cloak thrown over him. The triad of blues, greens, and golds may indirectly reflect the colors of a bright sunny day in central Russia. At the same time, the colors form a balanced whole. The luminosity of the colors adds a special charm to Rublev's masterpiece. When a ray of sunshine falls across the room in the Tretyakov Gallery where *The Trinity* is hung, the icon seems to wake up, blazing with a blue flame, and responds to nature's smile by giving off a light that eclipses everything around it.

In Old Russian art *The Trinity* is unique. The problems that faced Rublev in creating it are such that they can be solved only once. In the history of the arts there is no other one work that, to the same extent as *The Trinity*, embodies the best spiritual forces of an entire nation. If Rublev's *Trinity* were the only Old Russian painting to have come down to us, a thoughtful historian should be able to discern from it the whole culture of the people who created it—the character of this people, its ideals and aspirations, perhaps even its high destiny. The best sons of the Russian land brought together their precious gifts and handed them to Rublev, and he embodied them in his finest creation.

A number of works that have come down to us from the Moscow school bear the mark of Rublev's influence. An embroidered cloth with the figure of St. Sergey of Radonezh (plate 48) was apparently executed from drawings by one of Rublev's disciples. The portraitlike facial features of the saint are rendered here (this distinguishes it from later, more schematic portrayals). In the work of the woman who created this picture with her needle we can divine the character of the wise old man, his keen intelligence, his kindness and serenity, so different from the emotionalism and raptures of Theophanes' old men (plate 34). The composition is clear: the hair is balanced by the large beard, and within the oval face the lower tapering part is stressed—this articulation of forms is characteristic of Rublev.

The fifteenth-century Novgorod school developed parallel with the Moscow school and was partly influenced by it. Novgorod icons of the period are the more numerous in Russian museums. A large number of workshops in that town supplied icons not just to the city but

73. Saints Worshiping the Virgin
Embroidery. Late 15th century
Russian Museum, Leningrad

74. The Dormition of the Virgin
Embroidery. Late 15th century
Russian Museum, Leningrad

This embroidery is a masterpiece, both for the colorful execution of the saintly figures and for the quality of the lettered inscriptions. Some of these are embroidered in the medallions, others over the figures represented.

The Virgin is raising her arms protectively above the assembled saints. To her right is an angel; to her left, Moses. On the top border, on either side of the Redeemer, are two archangels and SS. Peter and Paul.

The standing figures include, on the right, three metropolitans: Alexey, Sergey of Radonezh, and Varlaam of Khutyn; on the left, Metropolitan Pyotr, Leonti, and Cyril of Belozersk.

In style close to icons of this period, this work follows the traditional iconography. Against a glory, Christ is lifting up the Virgin's soul, represented by the figure of an infant. The apostles are bending forward around the Virgin's body. On each side, near a ciborium, are saints who have come to worship the Virgin. Underneath the figure an angel is cutting off the hands of the disrespectful Avfonya, a scene frequently found in fifteenth-century icons. The insets show the Redeemer and the twelve apostles. They were added to embellish this cloth, which was made to be hung under an icon.

135

75 and 76. Walls and bell tower. *15th to 17th centuries*
Kremlin, Novgorod

The walls of the Novgorod Kremlin were built between 1484
and 1490. The bell tower, glimpsed here behind the wall, was
built in the sixteenth and seventeenth centuries.

The Kremlin has often been restored, the last time in the
nineteenth century.

also to the territories under its rule. The general technical level of Novgorod icon painting was very high.

Where the Moscow icons are characterized by their philosophical profundity, the Novgorod icons are more naïve and more plainly narrative. Rublev celebrated the love of mankind, whereas Novgorod icons delight and rejoice the eye, like a beautiful pageant. The Moscow icons are more subtle and refined, the Novgorod icons closer to popular taste. Echoes of folklore are noticeable even in objects destined for boyar purchasers. Democratic

After the victory of Ivan IV (known as Ivan the Terrible) over the Tatars and the capture of Kazan in 1552, the wooden Church of the Intercession of the Virgin was built in front of the Kremlin. A few years later, it was demolished and then replaced by a stone church surrounded by seven others in the form of towers joined by an arcaded gallery. The project was designed by the architects Barma and Posnik. The conception was highly imaginative and at the same time an obvious imitation of the many-domed and richly decorated pyramidal wooden churches.

The later addition of a chapel named after St. Basil accounts for the present name of the church. The cathedral has a polychrome decoration of painted brick and ceramic tiles.

forces always made themselves felt in Novgorod culture. With their characteristically practical outlook, the Novgorodians associated every saint with one or another field of practical life: St. George was looked upon as the patron of cattle breeders, SS. Flor and Lavr were patrons of horse breeders, St. Vlasii of cows, goats, and sheep. St. Nicholas was the patron and champion of the poor and unfortunate. The Novgorod masters were fond of legends and told them well. Their narratives are not only didactic but picturesque and entertaining.

The Novgorod icons are easy to distinguish from the Moscow ones; in the former, objects are clearly outlined, the contours mostly rectilinear and jagged. The favorite color of the Novgorod masters is bright cinnabar. The predominance of warm tones is stressed by contrasting them with cold tones, especially green. Novgorod icons always produce an impression of triumphant joy. Northern folk masters inherited their fondness for bright colors from the Novgorodians, as is apparent in embroideries and the decoration of spinning wheels.

In the beautiful fifteenth-century Novgorod icon *St. George and the Dragon* (plate 54), the warrior saint is shown thrusting his spear into the dragon's mouth, simultaneously galloping away from it and looking back. The struggle provides an occasion for suggesting the hero's valor, fearlessness, skill, and conviction of his righteousness. Hence the cheerfulness

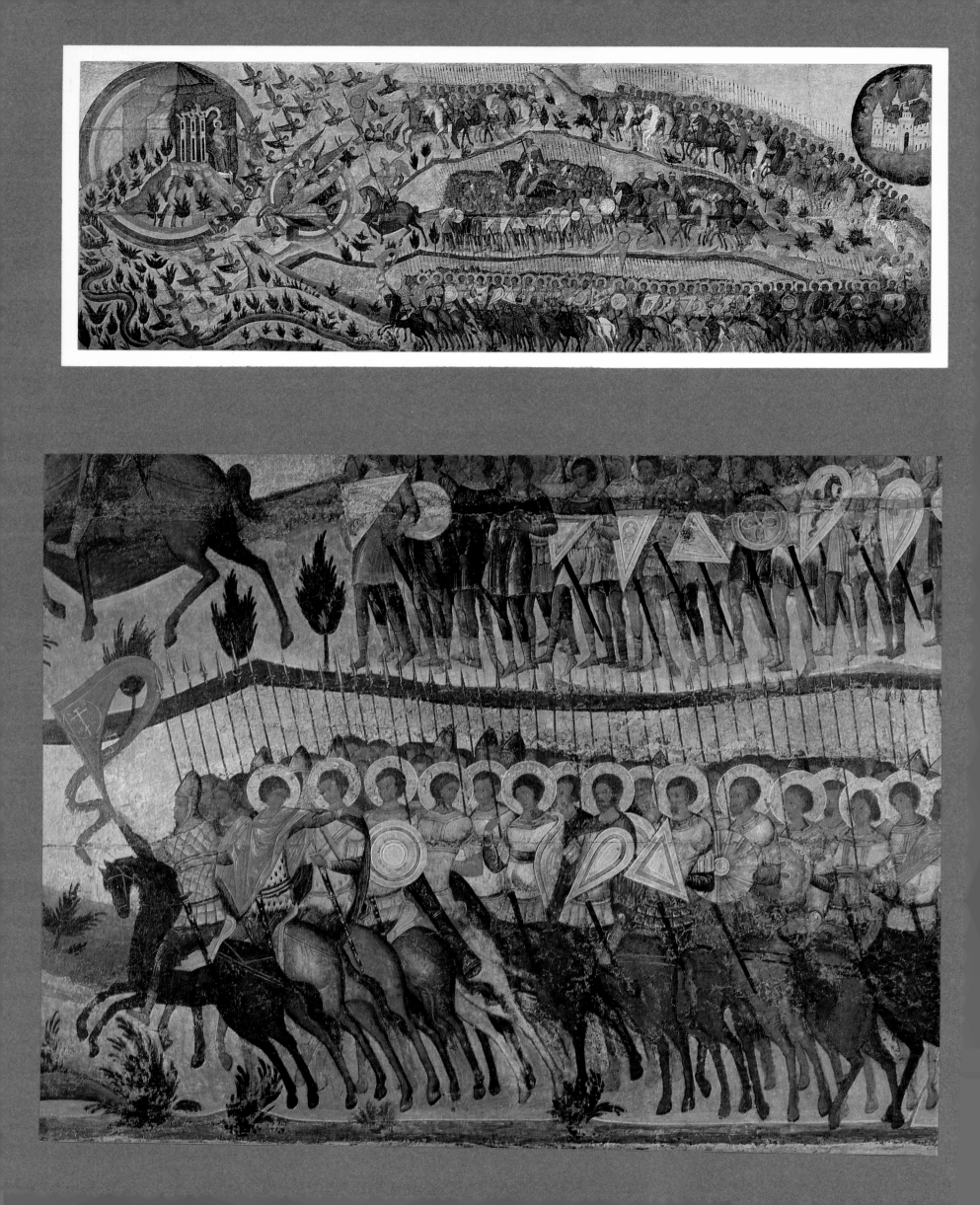

78, 79, and 80. The Church Militant
Icon. Mid-16th century
Egg tempera on wood, 56¾ x 156"
Tretyakov Gallery, Moscow

In 1552, Tsar Ivan the Terrible defeated the Tatar horde and captured the city of Kazan. It was a victory of the Cross over the Crescent. At the icon's right, in a circle of flames, is Sodom, which symbolizes Kazan. At the left, in a double glory, is the Heavenly City, in front of which the Virgin Hodegetria sits enthroned. This is an allusion to Moscow, which, after the fall of Byzantium in 1453, was regarded as the Third Rome.

Christ's armed horsemen advancing in triple rank toward the Heavenly City symbolize the Russian people, God's chosen ones, the "new Israel." This refers to a doctrine that arose in the late fifteenth century and developed under Tsar Boris Godunov.

In the top row of warriors Dmitri Donskoy is followed by his patron saint, Demetrius of Salonika, who rides a white horse.

In the middle row of warriors the Archangel Michael, surrounded by a glory and mounted on a winged red horse, is urging the warriors on. His head is turned toward Ivan the Terrible. Astride a gray horse, the tsar is holding high a red banner. Behind him, foot soldiers with shields are watched over by a man on horseback, who holds a scepter in the form of a cross: this is Vladimir II (Vladimir Monomakh). Above Ivan's head, three angels hold up Vladimir's tiara. (In the late fifteenth century, Vladimir was already regarded as "the greatest of the princes of Greater Russia." The story of his life was depicted in 1551 on the throne made for Ivan IV in the Cathedral of the Dormition in the Kremlin.) Around the Heavenly City a host of angels carrying crowns blessed by Christ are flying toward the warriors. Behind Vladimir Monomakh is a group of horsemen headed by Vladimir and his two sons, the martyrs Boris and Gleb.

In the bottom row, Alexander Nevsky, carrying a red banner, is riding in front of horsemen whose saintly character is indicated by their halos. St. George is just behind him. The horsemen carry shields, the blazonry of which has been partly deciphered.

This icon was found in the Cathedral of the Dormition in the Kremlin. In an eighteenth-century inventory it was called *Knights Blessed by the Almighty*, the words with which the office of vespers opened. It was given its present title in the twentieth century.

Parts of the icon, among them the circle of the city in flames and the group of warriors in the lower right-hand corner, were restored in the eighteenth century. These restorations have been kept because no earlier layer of paint has survived in these areas.

The blessed hermit is shown on a gilded seat next to the river Jordan. A heraldic-looking lion is holding out its paw, and the saint is removing a thorn from it. The black opening in the rock represents the hermit's cave. Behind the mountain we see a fortified town with gatehouse.

The style of this miniature icon ranges from the monumental to the familiar. The inscription reads: "St. Jerome and the lion by the river Jordan."

and joyful vitality of the icon. Like war songs, such icons arouse people to victory. The master treated the traditional type boldly, adjusting it to his own intentions. St. George's red cloak is normally the attribute of a martyr, but in this icon it spreads like a flame. His white horse is like the Pale Horse of the Apocalypse, but in this icon whiteness is a symbol of purity. The figure of St. George blends with the cloak, making the figure appear winged, the body arched like a tautly strung bow. The jointly turned heads of hero and horse, boldly rendered, hint at perfect understanding between them. St. George's shield, decorated with a mask, is like a solar disk, bringing out the movement of the figures by contrast. The master employed his allusions and exaggerations with great freedom. The icon fascinates us by its warm, sonorous colors. The dominant tones are bright cinnabar in the cloak and dazzling white in the horse. In the history of art we find many beautiful pictures of the dauntless knight, but one glance at the Novgorod icon gives us the certainty that he must be victorious, that his victory is as inevitable as the victory of light over darkness.

It has recently become clear that in the fifteenth century a number of Russian towns besides Novgorod and Moscow had their local schools of painting. So far they have been little studied. Here it is sufficient to mention that side by side with the Novgorod school of icon painting was the school of Pskov. Less artistic than the Novgorod school, it attracts us by its greater immediacy of expression. The Novgorod *Nativity* is characterized by clear, rigorous composition and balanced coloring. The Pskov icon *The Virgin's Assembly* (plate

82. Iconostasis
Detail of a royal portal. 16th century
Wood sculpture with traces of polychromy
Kiev Museum

The very low relief of this wooden door was carved with great care. It recalls the traditional wooden structures, with their rich geometric and floral ornament. In spots the original polychrome coloring is still visible. In the center of the panel is an icon showing St. John dictating to Prochorus on Patmos.

40) is pervaded with Dionysian passion, and its coloring is earthy, with dark greens predominating.

The remarkable icon *The Entombment* (plate 55) discloses a certain similarity in respect of coloring to the Novgorod manner. It may have originated in the north, but this is not provincial or folk art; like Rublev's *Trinity* (plate 47), it is the creation of a great master. The grief of Christ's nearest and dearest as they bend over the sarcophagus, Mary's despair as she presses against His body, the lifelessness of the figure of Christ swathed in its grave clothes—all this is rendered in the epic style of the icon. The bare, crystalline hills behind the figures look almost as though they have joined in the mourning. The woman with arms raised expresses the most intense grief at the same time that she performs a hieratic gesture. It is no accident that she is portrayed wearing a cloak of the most fiery red. The cinnabar fairly shrieks its despair. *The Entombment* should be compared with the somewhat later Novgorod icon *The Holy Women at the Tomb* (plate 56) to make us realize the difference between the masterpiece of a great artist, in which the form itself is meaningful, and the work of a minor artist, in which all the rules of painting are followed, yet which fails to move us. In *The Entombment*, the subject of death takes on universal human significance, as in Giotto's fresco at Padua on the same subject. But the epic expressiveness of this icon is even more reminiscent of the frescoes on Theban and Etruscan tombs.

This work is in a miniature style known as the Stroganov style. Savin was the personal painter of Maxim Yakovlevich Stroganov and also painter to the tsar. He worked in the late sixteenth and early seventeenth centuries. This icon recounts the life of Metropolitan Pyotr in twenty-four tiny scenes, each with its inscription.

In the center (not shown), Metropolitan Pyotr is gazing at the Virgin with the Christ Child in her arms. A group of the faithful is bowing down in veneration.

Among the twenty-four border scenes, which are grouped in pairs on two vertical panels, mention should be made of the most important episodes in the metropolitan's life. In 1305, he was appointed Metropolitan of all Russia by the Patriarch of Constantinople. Another scene shows him founding the Cathedral of the Dormition in the Kremlin in 1326. The last two scenes relate to his death and the discovery of his holy relics. In one of them we see a sailing vessel sent by Metropolitan Theognostes to inform the Patriarch of Constantinople of Metropolitan Pyotr's death; the crenelated walls of Constantinople can be seen in the distance. In the following scene, his relics are discovered. The backgrounds of the border scenes are decorated with a thin layer of gilded silver with floral geometric ornament.

On the reverse are two inscriptions in Slavonic, one giving the subject of the icon and the other the names of the owner and painter: "This icon belongs to Maxim Yakovlev, son of Stroganov, and was painted by Istoma Savin."

The icon was found in the funeral chapel of the Grand Duke Sergey Alexandrovich. The chapel is in the Monastery of the Miracle of the Archangel Michael in the Moscow Kremlin.

From the turn of the fifteenth century and throughout the sixteenth, under Ivan III and his successors, several cathedrals were erected inside the walls of the Moscow Kremlin, which now took on the appearance it has today. The Italians Aristotele Fioravanti and Alevisio Novi built the Cathedral of the Dormition (plates 1, 96) and the Cathedral of the Archangel Michael (plate 69). The Cathedral of the Annunciation (plate 58) was built by Russian masters. The Italian architects adhered to the traditional types of domed building, but the principles of Renaissance architecture, particularly the elements of the

This very beautiful embroidered cloth, the design of which is attributed to Theodosius, son of Dionysius, was executed in the tsar's workshop. It was commissioned by Vasily III prince of Moscow, and his wife, who were desperate for a male offspring. They donated the cloth to the Trinity-St. Sergey Monastery.

The Virgin, whose intercession is here invoked, is shown appearing to St. Sergey of Radonezh, the abbot of the monastery. The borders are decorated with a set of scenes of, among others, the Nativity, the Annunciation, and the Visitation.

The Trinity is represented in the middle of the upper border. To the left of this St. Sergey is holding his hands out to the Virgin in an attitude of supplication. The so-called Paternity theme is the subject of the border scene to the left of the Virgin: we see God the Father, the Son, and the Holy Ghost. At the foot of the cross is a dedication in beautiful Slavonic characters.

classical orders, which they applied, enriched Russian culture. The Kremlin edifices reflect the growing importance of the rulers of Muscovy and of the international position of the Russian state. In this decorous splendor, however, we detect popular sentiments in the many-domed churches, which embody a sort of dream of the heavenly Jerusalem. When we are inside the Kremlin, we see the various churches and bell towers as separate and distinct, but from a distance they blend, golden domes and all, to form one single gigantic temple surmounting the Russian capital on its hill above the river.

At the end of the fifteenth century an outstanding master, known as Dionysius, who was highly esteemed by his contemporaries, was active in Moscow. His art reflects the magnificence of the court of "the rulers of all the Russias," as the grand dukes of Muscovy began to be called. At the same time, Dionysius' art is characterized by great spirituality, elevation, moral purity—qualities that relate him to the Rublev tradition. In those days, autocracy was just beginning to pervade the exercise of governmental power, and art had not yet become a vehicle of official ideology. Like that of his great predecessor, Dionysius' painting is the high art of inspiration.

86. Trinity
Embroidery with silk and gold thread, pearls, and gold plates. 1599
Museum, Trinity-St. Sergey Monastery, Zagorsk

This is a work of both the embroiderer's and the jeweler's art. It was made at the Godunov workshop in 1599, and the Godunovs donated it to the Trinity-St. Sergey Monastery. The embroidery is attributed to Xenia, daughter of Boris Godunov. The cloth formerly hung under Rublev's icon *The Trinity*, which inspired this work.

Around the edges are small nielloed gold plates. The delicacy of their execution sets off the virtuosity of the embroidery in pearls. The angels' faces are the finest part of the embroidery.

In the middle of the upper border is the Paternity scene. The Virgin is at the left and St. John the Baptist at the right. In the center of the two vertical borders are (left) SS. Boris and Gleb and (right) two other saints. On the lower border are (center) St. Sergey of Radonezh, (left) St. Magdalene, and (right) St. Xenia.

Two large icons from the Cathedral of the Dormition, portraying the Moscow metropolitans Pyotr and Alexey together with episodes from their lives (plate 59), are probably early works by Dionysius. These metropolitans were revered by their contemporaries for having helped the grand dukes of Muscovy unify the Russian territories under their rule. Dionysius shows them both standing in brocaded chasubles with omophoria (this suggests a tendency to return to the pre-Mongol style). The episodes from the lives are treated in the same solemn manner. The metropolitan is always shown performing his duties, standing up straight, a figure universally respected in death as in life. He is the leitmotif in every episode, now wearing a monk's habit, now the metropolitan's vestments, but always possessed of inner dignity. Yet for all the solemnity of these scenes, they are poetic and warmhearted.

The episode of Sergey and Alexey conversing subtly characterizes Sergey as a humble monk addressing a petition to Alexey, who is seated on his throne and giving the other his blessing. The peaceful tenor of their conversation is well conveyed. Together with the building, the two seated figures evoke the *Trinity*—such "quotations" from Rublev's works

151

are frequent in Dionysius. The objects depicted are stripped of detail and rendered in luminous, translucent tones, the colors subtly harmonized. The unassuming subject of a conversation transports us to the world of essences.

The *Crucifixion* by Dionysius (plate 61) contains nothing new, iconographically. But he asserts his artistic vision here, and thereby rises above the drama. A similar interpretation of this subject can be found only in Renaissance masters, such as Antonello da Messina. The body of Christ on the Cross is supple and graceful, without physical contortion, His raised arms close to the position of an Orans. This Christ is not a victim of cruelty but the image of human beauty, almost a St. Sebastian. It is noteworthy that Dionysius treats every object in the picture as an element in the overall arabesque. The figures of the angels, of the Church and the Synagogue are far smaller than the others and rather resemble the petals of a flower. The tender, transparent tones of the colors also bring to mind a flower.

Dionysius' last works were frescoes (plates 62, 63) for the Church of the Nativity in the Therapont Monastery (1502). Most of the scenes are not from the life of the Virgin but illustrations of verses in her honor from the *Akathist Hymn*. This made it possible for the artist to paint solemnly joyful scenes, in which people surround Mary and sing her praises. There is little action, little dramatic tension in these scenes; with their tender blues, pinks, and emerald greens and clear, balanced composition, they plunge the viewer into a celebratory atmosphere.

In the fresco illustrating the verse "Thou art a wall to virgins," the graceful Mary inclines her head slightly and stretches out her arms; the girls she is protecting stand at her

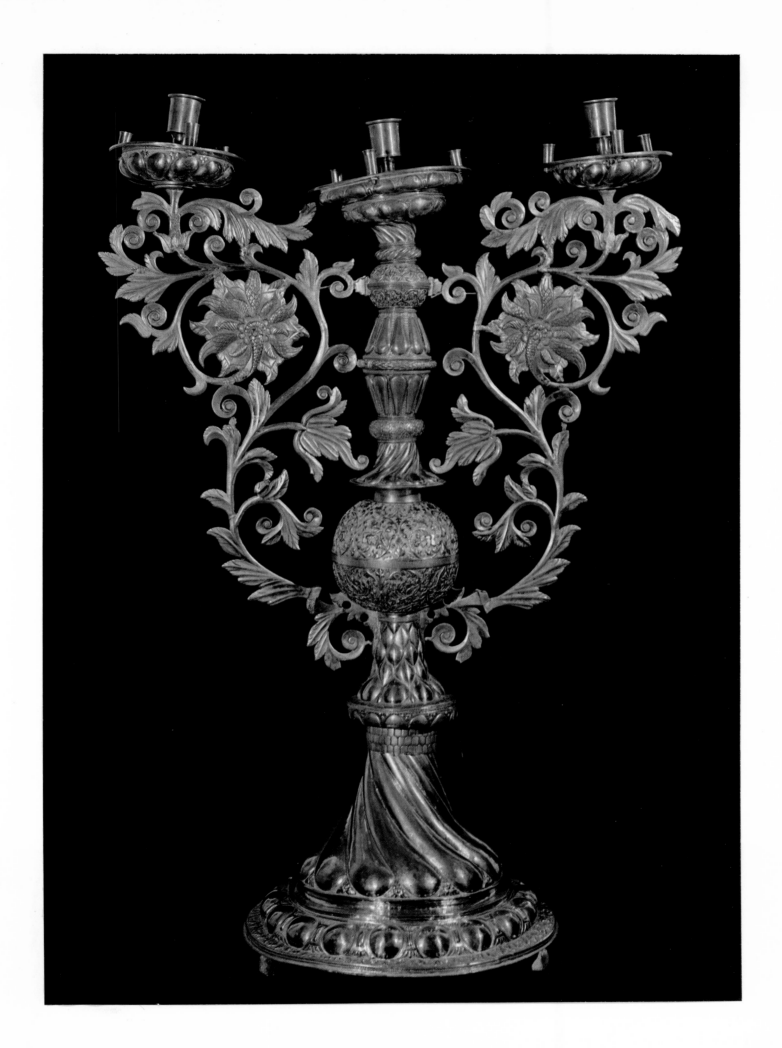

88. Covering for Rublev's Trinity
16th or 17th century
Gold, silver, enamel, precious stones, and pearls.
Museum, Trinity-St. Sergey Monastery, Zagorsk

Until 1904, this large work covered Andrey Rublev's *Trinity*. It is made up of several parts, made by Moscow goldsmiths in different periods.

The oldest part, a gift from Boris Godunov to the monastery, is the elaborately worked gold-leaf frame, embossed and engraved with figures and scenes, and encrusted with pearls and precious stones.

Tsar Mikhail Fyodorovich commissioned the goldsmiths of the Palace of Arms in the Kremlin to make the half-moon-shaped pendants over the breasts of the three angels. The tsar gave them to the monastery in 1626. The pendants are made of gold leaf encrusted with enamel, precious stones, and pearls.

In 1754, Rublev's masterpiece was completely covered with an additional revetment of gilded silver leaf.

right and left, and we can guess that they are singing a hymn in her honor. The stone enclosure is not a mere perfunctory attribute: the artist transforms it into an element of the composition. It indicates the depth of the little platform on which the figures are standing and at the same time is subordinated to the wall surface that forms a kind of frame around Mary. Dionysius was a past master at the art of translating words from Holy Writ into the language of pictorial images. Yet he did not confine himself to the translator's role. His frescoes are beautiful even without verbal commentary.

The remarkable icon *The Apocalypse* (plates 66, 67) was created in the Moscow Kremlin at the close of the fifteenth century. Nothing is known about the painter, who is referred to as the Kremlin Master. A study of his work shows that he owed a great deal to the Rublev tradition and is in no way inferior to his contemporary Dionysius but differs from him in that his imagination is freer and his gifts more dramatic in character. This artist was apparently familiar with the Judaizing heresy. Not for nothing did he creatively reinterpret the text of the Apocalypse. He may also have been familiar with Italian painting, although he adhered to his own traditions. In his infatuation with classical prototypes he went further than any other Russian master.

89. Chalice
Gold and precious stones. 1597
Museum, Trinity-St. Sergey Monastery, Zagorsk

The chalice is made of nielloed gold leaf and is studded with precious stones. It is engraved with delicate floral ornaments and insets. On the upper edge is the deësis: the Virgin, Christ, and John the Baptist. Lower down, in insets, are the four symbols of the evangelists. The meticulousness of the design is remarkable. The name of the donor, Boris Fyodorovich Godunov, is engraved on the foot of the chalice in beautiful Slavonic characters.

90. Iconostasis
Gilded wood carving. 1683—85
Cathedral of Smolensk, Novodevichi Monastery,
Moscow

This iconostasis was made by the famous wood-carvers of the Palace of Arms in the Kremlin. The archives of the Palace give full details of its construction. They mention several names, the chief of which is Osip Andreyev, and record the stages of the work, the materials used, and their cost.

The work was begun in the Kremlin workshops in 1683 but soon outgrew these quarters. The director of the shop, P. V. Sheremetev, therefore decided to set up other workshops in the Novodevichi Monastery. The iconostasis was not finished until 1685 except for a few details, one of which—the royal portal—was very important. The archives say that "two buckets of aqua regia were needed to mix the gold" and that "the gilding was done by Dorophey Zolotarev."

The royal portal was carved by Stepan. Although it was intended for another church, it had the right dimensions for the cathedral and was placed in the iconostasis. The icons, some of which were by the famous painter Simon Ushakov, were placed in the iconostasis, which today consists of five rows of icons. On the whole, the iconostasis looks just as it did when it came from the hands of the original craftsmen.

On the pillars in the foreground are sixteenth-century frescoes (the cathedral was built in 1524 in memory of the recapture of Smolensk, for which city it was named).

157

The Church of the Dormition was called Divnaya ("marvelous") because of its extraordinary beauty. It is the church of St. Alexey's Monastery, which was founded by Metropolitan Alexey in 1371 and burned by Lithuanian and Polish troops during the invasion of 1608–12. It was probably in memory of the men who died in battle that the church was built in 1628.

The church is surmounted by three pyramidal roofs crowned with domes. There are three apses behind the altar, continuing the triadic pattern.

This great icon in the Cathedral of the Dormition looks like a preliminary study for a monumental fresco. The artist included a great number of scenes in it, each clearly and individually characterized and arranged in sequence so that the narrative flows smoothly. At the same time, however, this enormous icon, with its several hundred figures, is self-sufficient and complete. It is an immense world created by the imagination of a great painter-poet.

He interpreted the text of the Apocalypse in his own entirely original way. He glosses over almost in silence the torments, disasters, and tragedies that his contemporary Albrecht Dürer immortalized in his woodcuts on the same subject. To the Kremlin Master, the Apocalypse is the promise of the kingdom of justice and love. Fear has been banished, and what the icon shows is a great number of scenes and figures depicting a utopia of human happiness, seductive beauty, yearned-for harmony.

His Horsemen are not agents of evil but sturdy heroes riding prancing steeds. The treatment of the horses brings to mind Paolo Uccello. The four angels of the Euphrates are not shackled demons but angels who resemble the classical Graces, harmonious and beautiful in the Rublev manner. The Kremlin Master possessed not only a vivid imagination but also great mastery, particularly in rendering crowds and movement. His colors are bright, joyous, transparent, luminous. With its numerous episodes the icon looks from a distance like a bright little meadow with flowers scattered over it.

92, 93, and 94. Monastery of St. Cyril of Belozersk, *Early 17th century*
Kirillovo-Belozersk

The monastery was founded in the fourteenth century by St. Cyril, a monk of the Simonov Monastery in Moscow. Therapont, the founder of the famous Therapont Monastery, was his contemporary at the Simonov Monastery. Attracted by the wilderness of northern Russia, they followed the example of St. Sergey of Radonezh in opening up this territory, where great centers of cultural and spiritual life would one day flourish. With his own hands St. Cyril erected the first wooden buildings—a small church and a hermitage for the first disciples.

The present buildings date from the early seventeenth century. They give the impression of an impregnable fortress. Within these walls were no fewer than seven hundred cells. The walls had twenty-three towers with slit windows of the type shown here.

Although the monastery was built in the seventeenth century, its architectural style is that of the sixteenth.

In the fifteenth century, at the same time as painting, embroidery developed in Russia. This is not a mere craft but a genuinely great art created by Russian women, a kind of painting executed with the needle instead of the brush. Nor must we suppose that the embroiderers merely imitated icon painters, taking icons and frescoes as their models. The embroideries disclose the same style as "great" painting. Perhaps more clearly than the icons and frescoes they reflect the decorative taste of the period. The fabrics disclose with particular clarity an ability to preserve feeling for the material employed. The Russian embroideries are pleasing not only for the scenes and figures portrayed, and not only for their beautiful colors, which are chosen with taste and form a harmonious whole, but also for their technique of execution, for the patterns that emerge from the interweaving of colored threads with gold and silver ones.

Earlier embroidered cloths, such as the Novgorod deësis dating from the beginning of the fifteenth century, seem to reproduce dabs of many shades and colors, contour lines—the form produces an impression of restlessness. In the cloth portraying *The Threnody* (plate 53), the contour outlining the body of Christ and the groups around Him is more clearly marked. In cloths dating from the second half of the fifteenth century, such as *The Dormition of the Virgin* in the Russian Museum (plate 74) and *The Miracle of the Archangel Michael* in Zagorsk (plate 72), everything is built upon the harmony of separately treated planes and very subtle color relations in the spirit of Dionysius. In the second of these, the inscription in big letters around the margin forms a pattern and serves as a frame. The cloth with the *Dormition* is surrounded by medallions of the saints, and there is even less sense of space. There is less heaviness in the figures, but the decorative element is stronger.

The last period of Old Russian art extends from the second half of the sixteenth century to the beginning of the epoch of Peter the Great. This period has several subdivisions. But to form a general idea of Old Russian art, it is indispensable to familiarize oneself with the motive forces of the age. Beginning with Ivan the Terrible, Russian autocracy grew stronger and stronger, its characteristic Oriental features of centralization and bureaucracy

95. Dome of the Church of the Consecration of the Priests. *1484–86*
Domes of the Cathedral of the Redeemer. *1678*
Kremlin, Moscow

The Church of the Consecration of the Priests, which was built by architects from Pskov, has only one dome, as does its model, the cathedral of the
Andronikov Monastery in Moscow. The façade is decorated with pilasters,
and the pointed arches give a lithe elegance to the upper part of the façade.
The general effect is one of great purity.

Behind this little church we see the golden cupolas of the Cathedral of
the Redeemer, built in the seventeenth century.

96. *Interior views*
Church of the Consecration of the Priests
Cathedral of the Dormition
Kremlin, Moscow

The four upper views show the iconostasis and frescoes of the Church of the Consecration of the Priests. This church was built in the late fifteenth century and was decorated with frescoes in 1644. The iconostasis dates from 1627. The icons are the work of N. Istomin, painter to the tsars.
The two lower views show the iconostasis and frescoes in the Cathedral of the Dormition. The frescoes were painted in 1642–43 by the most famous artists of the period.

ever more marked. The Church submitted entirely to the tsars and helped bolster their authority. Art lost its independence, submitted to the Church, was content to perform menial functions; purely illustrative, dogmatic elements became strongly predominant.

To evaluate the result one need only study the enormous icon *The Church Militant* (plates 78–80), executed under Ivan IV to commemorate the capture of Kazan. This icon is a monument of official art. Its dimensions are exorbitant and it is crammed with intricate symbols, both obviously dictated by those who commissioned it. It is a perfect clutter of objects. The execution is skillful, but dry. Obviously, subjugation of icon painting to the Church dealt an irreparable blow to artistic creation.

This is not to say, of course, that no beautiful works were created in Muscovy even after the sixteenth century. The old traditions remained strong for a long time. But painting became more and more didactic in theological and apologetic senses, less and less imaginative, vivid, and poetic. With increased deliberateness and restraint, it became ever more coldly official.

But it should not be supposed that autocracy and the Church managed to gain total control over the creative powers of the Russian people. During this same period, there were several popular uprisings against serfdom and the tsars. Stepan Razin's rebellion shook the Romanov monarchy. On the eve of Tsar Peter the Great's reforms, popular protest

97. Cathedral of the Trinity, Pskov. *1682–99*

The Cathedral of the Trinity, inside the Pskov Kremlin, stands on a height over the Velikaya River. This huge edifice looks almost exactly as it did when it was built.

took the form of a prolonged struggle between the defenders of the ancient rite and the official Church.

One essential characteristic of art in this era was that folklore began to infuse it with new life. Art was enriched by the products of popular fantasy and was made entertaining. Naturally, seventeenth-century works of this type attract our sympathy today. We need only compare the icon (probably of northern origin) of *St. Jerome and the Lion* (plate 81) with *The Church Militant* to realize how various were the tendencies in Russia in the period. This miniature icon is neither cold nor official but on the contrary reflects great warmth of feeling, directness, and poetic fantasy. Popular fairy tale elements also made their way into art at the turn of the sixteenth–seventeenth centuries, in the so-called school of Stroganov.

The popular element also influenced Russian architecture from the sixteenth century (Cathedral of St. Basil the Blessed, 1555–60, plate 77) to the early eighteenth century (the twenty-seven-domed Church of the Transfiguration on Kizhi Island in the Olonetsk district, plate 104). The wooden architecture of northern Russia is the direct offspring of the forest native to the region. Even outwardly the tent-shaped churches resemble tall fir trees. They are in unison, so to speak, with the nature around them. They breathe tremendous strength. Such edifices bring to mind the Russian peasant making his way, ax in hand, through the woods—clearing the ground, fencing off land, building towns, indomitably. In the north are most surviving examples of Russian popular sculpture, such as the

The majestic mass of this five-domed cathedral recalls the other Cathedral of the Dormition, in the Moscow Kremlin, which was built in the fifteenth century.

In 1684 it was decorated with frescoes by the best painters of the period. In the eighteenth century, the old roof with semicircular arches was altered to a simple roof sloping on four sides. The tombs of Tsar Boris and his family were found in the west part of the church. In 1781 this part, which had collapsed from age, was replaced by a narthex, and the tombs were transferred to another site. There is still a stone sarcophagus on the monastery grounds.

In the foreground is the small seventeenth-century Chapel of the Holy Well, built over a spring.

seventeenth-century icon of *St. George* from Archangel (plate 101), with its sense of narrative fantasy, rather stiff carving, sketchily suggested hills, and colors of the kind used in painted icons. Here traditional Old Russian iconography was preserved, but its most precious quality, its artistry, is altogether lacking. The Archangel icon is the work of a craftsman rather than of an artist.

The popular element is detectable in earlier works, particularly in certain ones from fifteenth-century Novgorod. At that time, however, there were skilled professional masters to modify the popular motifs. In the seventeenth century, popular art became completely divorced from professional art, and is characterized by clumsiness, barbarism, survivals of magic and superstition. It reflects the wretched condition of the peasant serfs cut off from the great cultural traditions.

One other feature of sixteenth- and seventeenth-century art should be mentioned— a feature that becomes especially strong toward the close of the seventeenth century. This is the influence of the West. Western influence led to the complete Europeanization of Russian culture in the eighteenth century, opening up new artistic horizons. But before Russia had fully entered upon the path of post-Renaissance European art, she had to

99. Bowl
Gold, pearls, and precious stones. 1618
Palace of Arms, Kremlin, Moscow

The bowl is in the form of a bird and is encrusted, both inside and out, with precious stones and rows of pearls. On the outside, between the stones, is an inscription in Slavonic. The bowl once belonged to Tsar Mikhail Fyodorovich (1612–1645), the first of the Romanovs.

100. Bishop's miter
Nielloed gold decoration encrusted with
precious stones and pearls. 1601
Museum, Trinity-St. Sergey Monastery, Zagorsk

This miter was a gift from Boris Godunov to the monastery.

This folk sculpture shows St. George on a horse, plunging his lance into the winged dragon's jaws. The landscape is composed of white rock; the blue at the lower left represents the sea. In the upper left-hand corner Christ appears in the clouds and gives his blessing. On the right is a building in Near Eastern style, with figures at windows and entrance.

The prepared lime wood was painted in tempera. This work comes from the Church of the Ascension in the village of Konetz-Gorye, in the Archangel area.

assimilate its elements, and this strengthened a certain spirit of compromise in seventeenth-century art. We see this most clearly in the decorations of the Yaroslavl churches. In some cases the seventeenth-century masters took Western engravings of the sixteenth and seventeenth centuries for their models, transforming the black-and-white originals into colorful, decorative frescoes. However, attempts to adapt Western forms to icon painting resulted in a syncretism and eclecticism such as had been unknown in the purer art of an earlier day. In decorating the churches in the Rostov citadel, the Russian masters borrowed from Western models but succeeded in preserving the decorative character of the fresco, the beauty of fluid contours, and a rhythmic style of composition.

The spirit of the epoch is especially clearly expressed in the jeweler's art, enamel work, embroidery, woodcuts, etc. Here Russian masters of the sixteenth and seventeenth centuries displayed the same decorative feeling that is apparent in seventeenth-century Russian architecture. In the Trinity-St. Sergey Monastery, one notes with what sure taste the tiny Chapel of the Holy Well (late seventeenth century) is set against the background of the stately sixteenth-century Cathedral of the Dormition (plate 98) with its smooth white walls. The tiny building looks in comparison with the other like a jeweled box you could almost pick up in your hand.

This decorative element holds sway in countless artifacts—there is a particularly rich

This small wooden church was transported from the village of Glotovo in the Yuriev-Polski region in 1960 and was set up not far from the Cathedral of the Nativity of the Virgin in Suzdal. This was the first step in the creation of an open-air museum of architecture (like the one at Kolomenskoye, near Moscow).

The church, which harmonizes perfectly with the surrounding landscape, is one of the few monuments of old wooden architecture surviving in this part of central Russia. It recalls the modest *isbas* (peasant houses) of the region. It has the same purity of line and is a product of the same fine workmanship. The origin of this form, at once simple and monumental, goes back to a very remote past. The same forms appear in the seventeenth- and eighteenth-century stone architecture of the Vladimir-Suzdal region.

Entirely of wood, the church has a covered porch running around three sides. On the east side is a small apse. The roof and the onion-shaped dome are made of small overlapping boards reminiscent of fish scales.

collection of them in the Palace of Arms (Kremlin, Moscow, plate 99). The artifacts of the period are not impressive just for the value of the materials used—made possible through the generosity of those who commissioned them—but for the inventiveness with which the masters made use of gold, pearls, enamel, precious stones, etc. Viewers unfamiliar with Old Russian art are usually stunned by the fabulous richness of these collections. Such treasures were used in former times to impress foreign envoys with the wealth and power of the Russian tsars. The generosity of the patrons, however, was not always compatible with good taste, nor is the magnificence of the objects always commensurate with their artistic worth.

What was happening to Russian art in the sixteenth and seventeenth centuries can be followed in embroidered cloths of the period. The fifteenth-century cloth with *The Miracle of the Archangel Michael* is very beautiful, thanks to the contrasts between the figures and the red ground, between the episode depicted and the inscription framing it, and to the four cherubs at the corners. The energy of the angel and the humility of the monk are

The church is part of a group of wooden structures on one of the islands in Lake Onega. Its style is in keeping with Old Russian traditions that were particularly respected in the north in the eighteenth century. Its pyramidal shape harmonizes with the flowing lines of the surrounding landscape. Like the men who wrote the epic northern poems, the architects and workmen responsible for this structure have remained anonymous.

A unity of effect was achieved by subordinating details to the whole. The monochrome of the natural wood, which has weathered over the years, creates a certain overall balance.

The shape of the church was very carefully devised. There are three superimposed octagonal prisms, the largest of which serves as the base. On four sides, square structures have been added, crowned by brace-shaped arcs known as *botchki* ("barrels"), and these are surmounted by small domes set on cylindrical drums. The twenty domes, arranged at four different levels, rise harmoniously toward the larger central dome that crowns the structure. This central dome symbolizes the Redeemer. One more dome has been set over the roof of the polygonal apse, on the east side. There is a large covered porch on the west side. The tent-shaped nave is decorated with a magnificent carved wood iconostasis.

here expressed as effectively as in the icons of Dionysius. In the cloth showing *The Virgin Appearing to St. Sergey of Radonezh* (1525, plate 85), the viewer's attention is focused on the Cross: all the figures appear to be bowing to it. Because the scene is small they blend with the border scenes. In the cloth with the *Trinity* (1599, plate 86), the picture has been entirely absorbed into the decorative design. The threads of pearls break up the central episode and the border scenes alike. Here skilled craftsmanship has crowded out inspiration.

In the seventeenth century, an Oriental type of design was widely used in decorating pottery. The whole surface was broken up into tiny parts; the classical principle of Russian art practically disappeared. Rublev's masterpiece was imprisoned in a golden revetment and covered with precious stones. This lavish, heavy suit of armor effectually hid from human eyes the work of the greatest Old Russian master. It is hard to say whether this was an example of Oriental vanity or of barbaric lack of taste.

Looking over the treasures of Old Russian art collected in this book, the reader will not confine himself to enjoying the beauty of individual works but will naturally ask more general questions. And first of all, is this art merely a local phenomenon, or does it deserve a place in the history of world art? We have not yet sufficiently studied the history of Old Russian art, its masters, and its various schools. Necessarily, our study has tended to make us isolate it from the art of other countries, so that it is hard for us to answer this important question. Even for a provisional answer, we must rise above minute details and concentrate on the finest achievements of Russian art.

There is no doubt that Old Russian art, and above all that of the fifteenth and early sixteenth centuries, when it attained independence and reached its flowering, should take its place in the history of world art. It belongs entirely within the scheme of artistic values created by the nations of Europe toward the close of the Middle Ages and during the Renaissance. At the same time that the Russian people were laying foundations for the national state, Russian artists were attempting to resuscitate those humanistic principles believed inseparable from the legacy of the ancient world. In the West the transition from the Gothic era to the Renaissance was abrupt; in Russia there was no need for so abrupt a change, for art had never broken away from the Byzantine, Greek tradition. In the West the Renaissance was based to a great extent on Roman art; the Russian masters from Rublev on were attracted by the early Hellenic tradition. They knew it mainly through Byzantine paraphrases, yet they correctly discerned its essential features: monumental grandeur, noble purity, clarity of outlines, rhythmic contours, and polychromy. Historical obstacles arose to prevent the development from continuing indefinitely. Russian art never achieved the cultural importance the Italian Renaissance has had for the whole world. The merit of Old Russian art is the extraordinary purity of its style and its character of sublimity. Its achievements cannot be forgotten by mankind. Our century may take pride in having for the first time recognized the true value of this remarkable legacy to world art.